working
for GOD

How to ... Study series

Series Editor:
TERRY VIRGO

working for GOD

RALPH TURNER

WORD BOOKS

NELSON WORD LTD
Milton Keynes, England
WORD AUSTRALIA
Kilsyth, Victoria, Australia
WORD COMMUNICATIONS LTD
Vancouver, B.C., Canada
STRUIK CHRISTIAN BOOKS (PTY) LTD
Cape Town, South Africa
CHRISTIAN MARKETING NEW ZEALAND LTD
Havelock North, New Zealand
JENSCO LTD
Hong Kong
JOINT DISTRIBUTORS SINGAPORE –
ALBY COMMERCIAL ENTERPRISES PTE LTD
and
CAMPUS CRUSADE, ASIA LTD
SALVATION BOOK CENTRE
Malaysia

WORKING FOR GOD

© Frontier Publishing International Ltd. 1993

ISBN 0-85009-625-1 (Australia 1-86258-290-4)

Unless otherwise indicated, Scripture quotations are from the New International Version (NIV), © 1973, 1978, 1984 by International Bible Society.

Created, designed and typeset by Frontier Publishing International Ltd., BN43 6RE, England. Reproduced, printed and bound in Great Britain for Nelson Word Ltd. by Cox and Wyman Ltd., Reading.

93 94 95 96 / 10 9 8 7 6 5 4 3 2 1

THANK YOU TO ...

Wendy McFee and Roger Flavell for the long hours they have put into the book, checking, changing and recommending. Special thanks to Wendy for her work on Chapter Six.

Kevin Wood for his helpful comments and agreeing to be the 'guinea pig' on the first draft.

Roh for the extra typing and Nathan and Elspeth for long term use of the homework desk!

Thanks also go to two long suffering secretaries, past and present, Pat and Jan.

Also available in the *How To* series:

FOREWORD

The *How To* series has been published with a definite purpose in view. It provides a set of workbooks suitable either for housegroups or individuals who want to study a particular Bible theme in a practical way. The goal is not simply to look up verses and and fill up pages of a notebook, but to fill in gaps in our lives and so increase our fruitfulness and our knowledge of God.

Both of Peter's letters were written to 'stimulate ... wholesome thinking' (2 Pet. 3:1). He required his readers to think as well as read! We hope the training manual approach of this book will have the same effect. Stop, think, apply and act are key words.

If you are using the book on your own, we suggest you work through the chapters systematically, Bible and notebook at your side and pen in hand. If you are doing it as a group activity, it is probably best to do all the initial reading and task work before the group sessions — this gives more time for discussion on key issues which may be raised.

Unless otherwise stated, all quotations from the Bible are from the New International Version.

Terry Virgo
Series Editor

CONTENTS

INTRODUCTION

When I was three, along with thousands of little boys before me, I wanted to be a train driver. It had something to do with the *Thomas the Tank Engine* books my Dad used to read to me.

By the time I was five, I had been given a set of plastic farm animals and nothing was going to stop me from becoming a farmer. That was, until our first school trip to the local farm. The smell! Suddenly a farmer's life seemed far less appealing.

By the time I was ten, I was centre forward for Manchester United Football Club, scoring goals alongside my childhood heroes, Charlton, Best and Law, (now doesn't that date me!) Upon discovering that I had two left feet, my thoughts turned to a tennis player, a pop star, a millionaire businessman — or maybe just a millionaire would do! I promised my Mum that by the time I was thirty, I would buy her a Rolls Royce. I did; it was a Matchbox version!

So often our childhood dreams fall far short of reality. I ended up as a Group Pensions Manager — and no one dreams of that profession!

The problem is, as Christians, we too have dreams which often fall short in reality. Upon conversion, we are encouraged to give all to God, to go for God, to serve Him 100 per cent. All of these are right motivations, but so often they are interpreted solely in the form of service within the church or of having a 'full-time call'. The fact is that most of us will not have a 'full-time call'. So how do we interpret our working hours in the light of God's Kingdom? What does God think about it? What does the Bible say?

A friend of mine once said that work was like new cars, pop music and expensive holidays. Somehow you felt that God ought to have an opinion on it, but you'd never managed to find out what it was!

I hope that by the end of this book you will have a new motivation and that you will see work not only as fulfilling, but as the call of God on a life.

Ralph Turner

Chapter One

IN THE BEGINNING

Peter reached out to turn off the alarm clock. It was that time again. Thinking back on yesterday, he wondered, for what seemed the millionth time, what work was really about. Why couldn't life be one long weekend? Football and friendship on Saturdays, great worship on Sundays. Surely that was real life. What possible relevance did his work have to enjoying life or serving God? Especially on a Monday morning.

Let's be honest, whether we're a manager, a shop floor worker, a housewife, teacher or computer programmer, whatever we do during our working hours, few of us can put hand on heart and say, 'I'm totally fulfilled in my job.' But when we understand God's opinion, we will begin to receive vision for our work. Then we will not only be able to cope with Monday mornings, but we will begin to enjoy our job more and, most importantly, use our day-to-day situations to serve God. We've already talked about being honest. Please be honest now in assessing how you see your job at present.

Most of the time my job is boring. I feel unfulfilled and underused.

I can't get excited about what I do. My job seems irrelevant to the world out there.

I hate my job. I would gladly give up tomorrow if I didn't have to pay the bills.

I enjoy what I do but find it difficult to see how God fits into it.

I don't enjoy my job much but am beginning to see that God is working with me.

I enjoy my job and am beginning to find ways of sharing my faith and of bringing God into my daily routines.

My job is fantastic. I feel totally fulfilled and couldn't think of any way of improving what I do.

WHAT DOES GOD THINK?

Now we've begun to assess our feelings about our jobs, we ought to consider how God feels about them. What is His attitude to work?

GOD WORKED FIRST!

The very first verse of the very first book of the Bible is about work. God created the heavens and the earth. It took Him six days. On the seventh day He rested. Why? Because for six days He had been hard at it! Even our heavenly Father had a weekly schedule.

MAN WORKED NEXT!

It didn't finish there. Having set the example, God then delegated various tasks to Adam, the first man. Genesis 1:28 and 2:15 describe the first three jobs assigned to man.

> Be fruitful and increase in number; fill the earth and subdue it. Rule over the fish of the sea and the birds of the air and over every living creature that moves on the ground.

> God took the man and put him in the Garden of Eden to work it and take care of it.

Read and meditate on Psalm 104.

Note the many mighty works of God. See in verses 23 and 28 how man's work fits in with God's plans.

It has always been God's intention for man to work.

Note in Isaiah 28:23–29 how God even instructs us in the practical duties we undertake.

There are many examples throughout the Bible of men and women who at one time or another worked for a living as part of their service to God: Moses and David were shepherds (Exod. 3:1; 1 Sam. 16:11); Peter was a fisherman (Matt. 4:18); Lydia was a cloth saleswoman (Acts 16:14) and Paul was a tentmaker (Acts 18:3).

Can you think of your own examples?

Hopefully, the exercise has helped you to consider Bible characters whom you might not normally have thought had occupations.

It is worth noting that it was because David served so willingly and successfully as a shepherd that God was able to prepare him to be a king. David was content in his task. He found time to worship God and perhaps compose many of the Psalms which were later recorded during his reign. Other examples, such as Paul, indicate a return to employment from periods of 'full-time' service. Others, such as Lydia, show no sign of any break in occupation. She simply continued to serve God through her work. So we see that God not only approves of men and women in occupations, but uses their employment for His own ends.

God wants us to work under His direction and to delight in what we do. He wants our work to reflect and continue His work and be honouring to Him. But things don't always turn out as He desires.

ADAM'S WORK

I once decided to grow some border plants from seed. I lost about half the seedlings from stem-rot, but realised that a dose of copper fungicide would keep the survivors. Many others died through lack of water over a particularly hot weekend when we were away from home. It intrigued me that despite the heat, a number of weeds had managed to germinate. In the end, only three plants made it to the border and two of those were all but demolished by slugs. So much for my gardening prowess!

My gardening experience is indicative of a much more serious garden experience in Eden.

Read about it in Genesis 3:1–19.

What were the main manifestations of sin in Adam and Eve's actions?

What aspects of sin do you think are seen regularly in your workplace?

God is a holy and just God who must deal with sin. In our work today, we are experiencing the consequences of God's judgement against sin. Genesis 3:17–19 says:

Cursed is the ground because of you; through painful toil you will eat of it all the days of your life. It will produce thorns and thistles for you ... By the sweat of your brow you will eat your food.

God worked on the garden and then gave the task of caring for it to Adam and Eve. He intended people to be his co-workers (1 Cor. 3:9) and to enjoy what they were doing. The consequence of sin was that work became a hardship, a curse. Our partnership with God was severed and we were promised lives of back-breaking toil, sweat and weeds. Not a day would go by when we wouldn't be dealing with the consequences of man's rebellion.

If that were the end of the story, this would be a very short book! Thankfully, there is another chapter. It centres around Christ's work on the cross.

CHRIST'S WORK

Psalm 103 sets out some of the amazing things that God has done for us. Although Christ was yet to come to earth, the Psalm points to His redemption.

> Consider verses 1–6 and note the seven things that God does for us.

Christ has not only given us eternal life in the future, He's given us a brand new here-and-now life too. This present life includes our employment. God wants us to become more like Him. He's preparing a bride (Rev. 19:7) and He will use our work to that end — the good and bad times. Work need no longer be meaningless to the Kingdom.

MEANINGLESS TO THE KINGDOM?

'I have my work and I have my church. The one is where I earn my living and the other is where I worship God. If I didn't have to do the first, I could do much more of the second.'

Have you heard that argument before? So often we introduce a secular/sacred divide. 'Church activities are the most important part of my life,' we say. 'Secular work takes second place.' But the divide is false. We don't suddenly become holy on Sunday mornings any more than we become secular on Monday mornings.

As John Loftness has said:

> Secular/sacred distinctions are wrong, but worse, they make 98% of Christendom feel cheap, tourist class and reserved purely for the outer courts.[1]

The apostle Paul wrote:

> Whatever you do, work at it with all your heart, as working for the Lord, not for men, since you know that you will receive an inheritance from the Lord as a reward (Col. 3:23,24).

If whatever we do involves serving Christ, it cannot be meaningless. It is a lie from another kingdom which says, 'Your employment is irrelevant to God's Kingdom.' If we listen to this voice, we will be in danger of trying to serve two masters — which is impossible.

If a Christian is at work, it is Christian work. Whatever we do is for the Kingdom — vacuuming the house, stamping pieces of paper, working machinery or selling newspapers — whatever our occupation, it is valuable to God.

It is not right to set one profession above another. A doctor's job may seem more important than that of an Inland Revenue clerk, but God doesn't view it that way. Paul's companion, Luke was a doctor and Jesus' disciple, Matthew was a tax collector.

Even God was not always involved in spectacular works. While He was creating the earth, He took time for what may be seen as the mundane work of planting a garden (Gen. 2:8). If God could ever get bored, He must have come pretty close to it when He provided daily manna in the wilderness for forty years! (Exod. 16:4).

I was recently at a conference where I heard a very moving testimony from a Chinese pastor who had been imprisoned for his faith. Because the authorities knew he was a Christian, they gave him the very worst jobs to do. His main employment was cleaning out the human refuse tank whose contents were used for fertiliser on the fields. To do this he had to get inside the tank. But he loved his job. For eighteen years he worked 'as ... for the Lord' (Col. 3:23). He found that because the smell was so overpowering, no one would come near him — including the guards. So he was able to sing gospel hymns at the top of his voice and no one would shut him up. He testified that for him, that human cesspit became his garden where he worshipped as he worked. His favourite hymn was this:

> I come to the garden alone
> While the dew is still on the roses
> And the voice I hear falling on my ears
> The Son of God discloses
>
> And He walks with me, and He talks with me
> And He tells me I am His own
> And the joy we share as we tarry there
> None other has ever known.[2]

Take time now to pray that your workplace will be like a beautiful garden for the Lord.

Consider three or four of your major functions during your working hours and pray individually about each. Now give them to God and ask Him to help you to see in each area that you are serving Him and that what you do is of great value to Him.

OUR HEAVENLY EMPLOYER

There are no meaningless occupations to God. He sees no sacred/secular divide.

Read James 1:6–8 and note what we are encouraged we can serve.

Read Matthew 6:24 and note how many employers we can serve.

Wherever our work, we have a Heavenly Employer. J.B. Phillips in his paraphrase of the Bible translates Colossians 3:23 as follows:

> Whatever you do, put your whole heart and soul into it, as into work done for the Lord, and not merely men ... you are actually employed by the Lord Christ and not just by your earthly master.[3]

Think for a moment of your immediate superior. Then think of his/her boss, then the boss above that. However big the company, you will eventually end up with the Managing Director or Chairman. Now recall that they were born, went to school and started work just like you. The Bible says that God appoints kings and rulers lifting some up and bringing others down (Job 24:23–24). Our employer is ultimately a heavenly one, interested and involved in all we do.

Martin Luther said:

> God works at common occupations. God is a tailor, who makes a coat for the deer which lasts for a thousand years. He is a shoemaker, who provides boots the deer will not outlive. He is also a butler who sets forth a feast for the sparrows and spends more on them annually than the total revenue of the king of France. And if God does these things, then surely we can honour Him in these humble callings also, and in many others besides.[4]

For most of us, our job will be God's calling on our lives — and we can't ignore it. Our work must reflect His. He is our Heavenly Employer — and we must remember that as we roll out of bed on a Monday morning.

[1] John Loftness, *People of Destiny Magazine*, Vol. 5:No.4. Used with permission.

[2] Written by C. Austin Miles (1912).

[3] J.B Phillips, *The New Testament in Modern English*, Revised edition, Harper Collins (1958).

[4] Martin Luther, as quoted by Michael Griffiths in *Consistent Christianity*, IVF Press (1960).

Chapter Two

INTO THE GRIND

It's 9.00 a.m. on Monday. Peter is at his desk. The papers are piled high. The two jobs he left on Friday afternoon still need finishing. He knows that his employer is ultimately the Lord, but how does that relate to finishing these (rather boring) jobs for his (rather unsympathetic) boss?

IT'S NOT ALL EVANGELISM!

If everything we do as Christians is for God, how do we apply this knowledge to our day-to-day situations? One of the keys is not to think that we have always got to be evangelising our colleagues. Too often we argue that if we are not successfully telling others about Christ, we are failing God. Evangelism has its place, as we will see in Chapter Eight, but work is good for its own sake.

> Read Ephesians 1:3–14 and note God's purpose in
> saving us in verses 6, 12 and 14.

By acknowledging God as our employer in the way we work, we bring Him glory — even if we don't open our mouths.

IT'S A GIFT

When we are released from the pressure of thinking, 'My only purpose at work is to evangelise' we will begin to relax and enjoy our job. This will then promote a right attitude to work — which will be to God's glory.

Note the attitudes to work in Ecclesiastes 5:18–20.

Work is seen as satisfying, the gift of God. An earlier passage, Ecclesiastes 3:13 supports this view:

> That everyone may eat and drink, and find satisfaction in all his toil — this is the gift of God.

The passage also sets out a very practical reason for working — survival!

What other reasons can you think of (e.g. it brings in finance)?

John Houghton gives his assessment of work:

> Work should have its reward. This is much more than merely a pay-packet. It is unfortunate that our society has so limited the concept of reward. Job satisfaction needs to include a sense of achievement, of producing something worthwhile, of creative expression, of appreciation by others.[1]

Many of us have had a limited view of work and must take time re-educating our minds. God wants us to see His creative work and to view ourselves as His co-labourers. He wants us to serve in such a way as points people to Him — whether or not we are able to share the gospel verbally. He wants us to view our work as a gift — and that will make a difference to the way we approach the daily grind.

As we begin to deal with some more practical issues, don't just amass information, pray the issues through and let your Heavenly Employer speak not just into your mind, but into your heart as well.

SOUND STARTING PRINCIPLES

If our daily occupations involve working for God, what are some of the underlying principles which will help make a difference? We'll focus more closely on some of them in Chapter Eight, but for now let's look at three interrelated practical areas.

SLEEP

It's obvious: if we are not getting enough sleep, our work will be affected. If we think very little of our work, we may not think our tiredness is a problem, but lack of sleep and poor quality of work can become a vicious circle.

> Read Proverbs 10:5 and note how God views sleep when there is work to be done.

> Read Ecclesiastes 5:12 and consider how God views sleep after a hard day's work.

Whenever I work in the garden all day or decorate the house, I have a 'wholesome tiredness' and my sleep that night will be very satisfying. However, if I cheat my employer of the best of my work because of tiredness caused by late nights, then it is likely that my night's sleep will be fitful. If we have a bad attitude to our work and see it as unfulfilling, we are likely to slip into patterns of permanent tiredness. A godly attitude to our job can free us in other areas of our life.

FITNESS

> According to 1 Timothy 4:8, of what value is physical exercise?

> In 1 Corinthians 6:19,20, what is our body described as and what are we to do with it? If we are not looking after our physical body, are we obeying this Scripture?

Now consider a few practical questions:

How often do you exercise?

If you feel you should do more exercise, what will you do, and when?

Are you at a reasonable weight for your height/ age? (If you are married, ask your spouse!)

If you feel overweight, don't just start dieting; share the problem and pray. If you are not careful, a diet can become more of a problem than your original weight. So be sensible and set achievable targets. Godly eating habits and appropriate exercise will enable us to cope with the pressures of our employment (see Chapter Five). But in the end these things are only of some value, so keep them in proportion.

TIME-KEEPING

As Christians we will be honest with our time-keeping. Lunch breaks will last an hour, unless we have permission. We will always arrive on time in the morning — except when there are unavoidable difficulties like traffic problems. Leaving early will be the exception, not the rule. We will take days off sick because we are sick. Our company boss may not notice these things, but our Heavenly Employer will.

If we are working at or from home, or are self employed, we may need extra discipline to ensure that we work the allotted number of hours.

AWKWARD MOMENTS

How do we deal with some of the more difficult day to day issues that we face in our employment? Here are four of the most common problems.

1. DEALING WITH THE OPPOSITE SEX

Let's start with the good news: Sex is great — in a marriage. With a strong marriage, we can face sexual temptation confident that God will help us. We can be clear about our working relationships with the opposite sex. However, temptations will still come our way, and married or not, we need to be aware of the dangers.

Most of the time, dealing with someone of the opposite sex at work may cause us no problem at all. But on occasions, a Christian man may encounter a woman who dresses with 'a view to a kill' rather than with a view to what is reasonable in a workplace. Similarly, a Christian woman may have to deal with the amorous approaches of some of her male colleagues.

Most of the answer lies in an awareness that these sorts of issues may arise and prayerful advance preparation for them.

Particularly for men, this is an area where both preparation and accountability are key. Preparation includes having a sober assessment of our weaknesses and ensuring a regular time with God — preferably before we go to work. We must be sensible about the possible temptations and not be over spiritual in our ability to cope with them. If we start each day with the One who can help, then we can turn away from the temptations as they arise.

Maybe the men need an extra word on not being over spiritual. It's a bit of a generalisation, but the average male can be quite a big-head! Don't assume that because you are happily married, or enjoying a good relationship with God, that you will be unshakeable in this area. Sexual liaison in the workplace is one of the major battle grounds for the Christian today. It is so easy to get involved with a work colleague — particularly if you are working on a project together. The sense of camaraderie can easily slip into something more. So beware! Proverbs 5:3–4 says:

> For the lips of the adulteress drip honey [sweet, delightful, strengthening], and her speech is smoother than oil [soothing, healing, she understands me....]; but in the end she is bitter as gall, sharp as a double-edged sword.

Accountability to someone of the same sex outside the workplace is another safeguard. Maybe you could talk and pray with your pastor, (or for the women, the pastor's wife), or your housegroup leaders. Traditionally, sex and money are two areas we don't talk about much. This needs to change.

Finally, if we are enjoying our job, that in itself is a safeguard. If we are where we should be and involved in what we are doing, there is less possibility of our minds or eyes wandering in other directions. David was a mighty man of God but because he was not where he should have been — out on the front line of battle — his eyes strayed Bathsheba's direction. Adultery and murder were the result (see 2 Samuel 11 and 12).

At this point, be honest with yourself:

Am I weak in the sexual area?

If so, are there any specific people at work I need to be careful of?

Am I organising my day to day work in such a way as to avoid temptation?

Am I regularly reading God's Word as preparation for the day of temptation?

Am I making myself accountable to someone I can trust?

God has given us sex to enjoy within the bounds of marriage. He has also given us work to enjoy. Genuine platonic friendships with the opposite sex in the workplace are not only possible; they are desirable. If we are married, we need to keep the relationship strong. But whether we are married or not, we need a realistic assessment of our weaknesses and an openness to God and to friends we can trust.

2. DEALING WITH BLASPHEMY

How do we respond to profanities, swearing and distasteful jokes? So many people use the Lord's name in vain and don't even realise it. One of the great things about being a Christian is that people notice, even when we do not say anything. We should be pleased when someone tempers their language when they that notice we are around. They have recognised something, or rather, Someone different in us.

But there will be occasions when it is right to confront colleagues, especially when they are blaspheming. Be polite but firm. Try and speak to them when others are not listening, in order not to bring embarrassment. Gently explain (Prov. 16:24) that their swear word is the name of Someone who is important to you. Leave the results with God. Sometimes you will win a friend, on others, a bit of healthy persecution!

3. FRIDAY LUNCHTIMES

Not every workplace has this problem but many people think that Friday lunchtimes are an opportunity for winding down before the weekend. But do their bosses see it that way? Surely, there are another three or four hours to go before the end of the working week. The charity, Alcohol Concern, estimate that in an average year in the UK fourteen million working days are lost due to alcohol absenteeism. In a survey of over 300 companies, there was strong support for a ban on drinking during working hours. That, of course, must apply to the company boardroom as well as the pub.

So how should Christians respond? The Bible does not have any one view on an issue such as drinking. Jesus drank wine and even changed water into wine (John 2:1–11) and Paul encouraged Timothy to drink moderately for the sake of his health (1 Tim. 5:23). However, we are warned against getting drunk (Eph. 5:18).

> Note what Ephesians 5:18 recommends as the alternative to being filled with drink.

If we are meant to enjoy our jobs, this must include a social aspect which may well include the odd Friday lunchtime. However, let's enjoy the friendship and company of our colleagues, without stealing hours from our employer. (We could even take the initiative and arrange a social function at another time.) As always, we need to be as shrewd as snakes and as innocent as doves (Matt. 10:16).

4. OFFICE POLITICS

Ambition, profit making, laziness and careless attitudes can lead to poor relationships among workers in their workplace. This creates a bad atmosphere. In situations where one party is trying to pull you one way and another party in the opposite direction, it is useful to remember the identity of our real Boss.

Philippians 2:3–5 says:

> Do nothing out of selfish ambition or vain conceit, but in humility consider others better than yourselves. Each of you should look not only to your own interests, but also to the interests of others. Your attitude should be the same as that of Christ Jesus.

We must adopt Christ's attitude. That means being free from our own selfish ambitions and making the interests of others our priority.

How does your attitude compare with Christ's in your own work situation?

Check your motives.

Pray for the person who most gets on your nerves.

If we have Christ's attitude, we should not get involved in many disputes and will particularly avoid gossip. But when problems do arise, we can pray into them and rejoice when God answers. The atmosphere of our workplace can be affected by prayer and our quiet witness (see Chapter Eight). There may be occasions when intervention is right — but let's always check our motives.

Another of these important issues concerns our day to day relationship with the boss.

DEALING WITH THE BOSS

In Chapter Four we will look at the manager/employee relationship through the manager's eyes. Here we will focus on the worker's attitude towards the boss.

ATTITUDE

The terminology used by Paul and Peter is that of slave/servant and master. Nevertheless, I believe it is legitimate to interpret these comments in the context of employee and employer:

> Read Ephesians 6:5,6 and note:
>
> What characteristics we should demonstrate in our dealings with the boss.
>
> Whose will we are ultimately doing.
>
> Read 1 Peter 2:18 and consider whether we are only to show these characteristics when our boss is reasonable.
>
> If you have the time, read the wider passages from which the above quotes are taken (Eph. 6:5–8 and 1 Pet. 2:18–23). They contain truths which fly in the face of much twentieth century thinking.

In this age of profits and losses, turnover and shareholder dividends, bosses often show little concern for employee welfare, care and quality of environment — unless it is related to financial gain. Today's increased reliance on technology can result in redundancies. Rarely are those who lose their jobs given the opportunity of ongoing contact and care from their former company. If we remember who our real Boss is, we will not react in an inappropriate way.

REACTIONS

Do we react? In all circumstances? What about times when too much is expected of us, or when we're ignored and others are preferred, or when we lose our job? Scripture is clear. We trust our Heavenly Employer.

> Read Titus 2:9,10 and consider:
>
> What we should try to do for our employer.
>
> How we should react.
>
> The reaction that our good behaviour should provoke in our employer.
>
> What else should become attractive to him.

Being ignored when others are being preferred is a common experience. Daniel sets us a good example in this respect. He was a man of God working in the world. Babylon was the centre of worldly civilisation and as a captive, Daniel didn't want to be there — how often do we feel like that about our jobs! But he was also ready to work for God and that work brought him both great acclaim and great persecution (Dan. 6:16,19). Whatever the results of his work, Daniel was not willing to compromise and do things the world's way. He accepted promotion when it came, but he also faced up to the hard times, preferring God's recognition to that of the king.

> Look again at Colossians 3:22–25 and remind yourself where your reward is and whom you are actually serving.

Although our earthly boss may show favouritism, there is no favouritism with God. That is our security, our identity — it is rooted in Him. We are ultimately God-pleasers, not men-pleasers and even if our boss does not notice what we do, we can be assured that God does.

> **Therefore, my dear brothers, stand firm. Let nothing move you. Always give yourselves fully to the work of the Lord, because you know that your labour in the Lord is not in vain (1 Cor. 15:58).**

There is a difference, though, between trusting our Heavenly Employer and ignoring injustice. There may be occasions when reaction is the correct response.

Consider an occasion when Jesus reacted strongly. What were His reasons for doing so?

**When might it be appropriate for you to react at work?
How might you do this?**

BREAKING THE RULES

Normally, our reaction should be not to react. But what happens when we're asked to break the rules? What if we're told to quote a delivery date we know won't be kept? What if our boss expects us to tell a customer that he's out when he's definitely in?! What if we're taught to exaggerate the benefits of a product? Lies, exaggeration and compromise are a minefield for the Christian! We must stand strong in this area. There can be no compromise with the truth.

> Read 1 Thessalonians 5:22 and note what we are to avoid.

We must deal with this problem with tact and diplomacy. If you can, approach your boss privately to avoid embarrassment. Then speak clearly but with respect. The result will often be an apology on his part. If it is not, we need to remember again who our real Boss is. Daniel was tactful and reverent towards the king, but he showed not the shadow of compromise.

> Turn to Daniel 3 and read the first 18 verses. Note the careful way in which Daniel's three friends speak to the king in verses 16 to 18.

They know they don't have to defend themselves should the king react. Even the threat of death will not deter them from serving God. In this particular story, God answered in dramatic fashion but even if He hadn't, the three would not have changed their minds.

We cannot compromise with lies. What today is only a bit of exaggeration, tomorrow becomes something more. Today it may just be false delivery dates but tomorrow it may be false accounting or worse. Most companies are honest. Most bosses are reasonable. But even if we lose our job, we must keep our faith.

> Read 1 Peter 1:6,7 and note how our faith is proved genuine and what its result will be.

Our employment is a gift from God, so He is perfectly entitled to take it away. We are called to stand for righteousness, and must leave the consequences of our actions with Him. If we lose our job because we refuse to be dishonest, He probably has something better for us in store.

---

[1] John Houghton, *Issues Facing Society*, School of the Word series, Harvestime (1988). Used with permission.

Chapter Three

AM I IN THE RIGHT JOB?

He's wearing the latest Italian silk suit; not a hair out of place; no dandruff on the collar; perfect creases in his trousers. His tie is straight, his breath fresh and he smells of expensive aftershave. The work papers under his arm are neatly collated into a brand new folder. As he leans over his female associate's beautifully polished desk (with not a pile of papers in sight), there is a warm smile on his face. She looks up, delighted to see him, her teeth gleaming, as she reaches for her 100 per cent decaffeinated coffee. Does it sound like your workplace? Mine neither!

This carefully manicured executive image belongs only to the TV screen and the advertising world of banks (how come they never smile at me like that when I call?!), building societies, airlines and, of course, coffee producers. It's not the real world and it's not surprising that young people in their first job quickly become disillusioned.

So what should we expect? What's the choice? If we are already in work, is it the right job? Does it live up to our expectations? Are we stuck in a rut? What if we never seemed to make a choice? Let's look at the different types of jobs and areas of work available, both from the point of view of someone starting out and for those of us already in employment.

Jobs change. We change. It may be that what was the right decision five years ago needs questioning now. On the other hand, it may simply be that we need to let God do a work in us and our attitudes.

FREEDOM TO CHOOSE?

In some societies, there simply isn't a choice. We need to thank God for the freedom we have which allows for the possibility of job changes. For some of us there may genuinely not be any choice right now, perhaps because of the limited availability of jobs. You are not alone. Many people in New Testament days did not have a choice. Job opportunities then were few and far between and the son was often expected to follow in his father's footsteps. Jesus did that, following his father's trade until He was thirty years old.

> Read 1 Corinthians 7:20–22 which is in the context of slavery and freedom.

> Note whether Paul indicates the possibility of changing employment.

> Read Ephesians 6:5–8 and Colossians 3:22–24. Do we always have a choice?

I want to challenge the all too common assumption that there can be no change to the mundane employment that we may be doing. God has a purpose for our working hours and a change of job is well worth considering. Having said that, let's make one thing quite clear: a job change is not the automatic solution to a lack of fulfilment.

We live in an age where 'self fulfilment' has become a god (see the New Age section of Chapter Seven). As Christians, we can expect to suffer for our faith (1 Pet. 3:13,17; 4:16) and it may be that this suffering manifests itself in the workplace. Our job fulfilment is in the context of serving Christ and our job satisfaction may have to be similar to that of the Chinese pastor mentioned in the first chapter. He was fulfilled and content with his task. It brought about perseverance (Col. 1:9–11) and drew him close to God. But if someone had offered him a change of employment, I guess he might have taken it!

Too often, the Christian message is watered down to one of 'God will bless you.' The biblical message is that for Christians there will be suffering and trials. We will have to contend with weeds. Work will be by the sweat of our brow. But the fact that Christ has redeemed us will affect our attitude to the workplace even if it does not affect what we actually do. By God's grace, we may end up with a job that we thoroughly enjoy. Alternatively, we may have to suffer and find fulfilment and contentment despite the ongoing circumstances.

Read again 1 Corinthians 7:20–22.

Although a slave is encouraged to gain his freedom if he can, he must not let his situation trouble him.

Read John 4:31–34 and note the source of Jesus' fulfilment.

Although there are times when it is right to stay in a job despite the circumstances, we must not make this fact an excuse for laziness in not looking for alternative work. The verses used to encourage someone to stay in certain employment often refer to slaves and masters. We have already concluded that it is safe to apply these verses to today's situation. But we should also note that, unlike New Testament days, we are unlikely to lose our lives if we try to change our circumstances!

HOW TO CHOOSE

Most of us can choose our career — and the choice is vast. In Chapter Seven we will look at a few areas that we must avoid. Here, we will consider how we go about choosing what we do.

COMMON SENSE

God has blessed us with common sense and we ought to use it! Peter encourages us to:

> be of sound judgment and sober spirit (1 Pet. 4:7, NASB[1]).

So let's start to think through the issues. If you are unsure about your job or future career, first assess your strengths and weaknesses. What do you feel drawn to? What do you enjoy doing? What motivates you? What would you get out of bed on a Monday morning for?

Do you enjoy working alone or with people? Are you mechanically minded or do you prefer holding a pen in your hand? Is your best friend a calculator, a computer screen or a crossword? It is amazing how many people have never carried out this sort of 'obvious' exercise and then wonder why they are in a job that they don't enjoy.

Assessing your strengths and weaknesses is big business. For a few pounds, you can buy a simple do-it-yourself question and answer book which will help you analyse your own character and abilities. For a few hundred pounds, you can take yourself away for a day of psychometric testing. Provided we use our common sense in realising the limitations of such testing (and, occasionally, the dangers of New Age influences in some of the more convoluted and cranky practices), we can discover some positive indicators of our abilities and aptitudes. As David Frahm has said:

> We aren't blank slates on which any old inscription can be engraved. Job matching is not simply a function of acquiring a title and necessary skills to go along with it. We're predisposed to a particular direction; we have an aptitude for a particular style of functioning in

our world; we are motivated by the dreams and desires for contribution that have been planted deep within us.[2]

Read Romans 8:9,28 and consider how we have been 'predisposed to a particular direction.'

Read 1 Corinthians 2:16 and note whose mind we have.

As we stay close to God, we can trust our common sense on what job to pursue.

Read Proverbs 11:3 and note the fate of those who are unfaithful to God.

Note also what should characterise our lives if we want to have clear guidance.

To help you determine your strengths and skills, consider to what extent the following statements are true of you. You may wish to score yourself on a '–3 to +3' scale according to how much you agree with them. Your answers may suggest whether you are in the right job.

Calling
I feel drawn to my profession. It stimulates and challenges me. I look forward to starting work each day.

Characteristics
My known character traits suit my job well. Although at times I must work hard, most of what I do comes naturally to me.

Confirmation
My friends and family think that I am good at my job. My work colleagues think well of me. My boss thinks I do a good job. This view is reflected in salary rises, appraisals and promotion.

Contentment
Most of the time, I am happy in my job. At the end of the day, I feel satisfied with what I have achieved. I do not usually find my job stressful.

If your total score is on the plus side, however slight, it is likely that you are in the right place, unless there is clear guidance to the contrary (which you must check out with others). If your score is negative, it may be that you seriously need to consider a change.

If you have found this exercise helpful, you may like to follow up your findings with some further, more refined tests. Most good book shops will have an assortment of these. One with a particularly Christian viewpoint is *The Great Niche Hunt* by David J. Frahm, published by Navpress. As well as providing some useful teaching on the subject of job changes, it gives you a number of practical exercises to complete. The intention is that by the end of the book you will have a good understanding of your God-given strengths and weaknesses.

You may well find a correlation between your job strengths and your spiritual strengths. This should not be surprising if you remember that there is no distinction between sacred and secular.

OTHER PEOPLE'S SENSE

Hopefully, if you are starting out on your first job you will have received help from your career's officer at school or college. If not, an interview at the local job centre may be a good way forward. This could be combined with a trip to the reference library which usually carries a wealth of information on different occupations.

God does not call us to Himself and then leave us to get on with it. We have His individual guidance (which we will consider in more detail in a minute); He also puts us in a family. Our brothers and sisters are there to bless us. We should never make a major change in our lives without seeking the wisdom and advice of others and praying it through with them. Our own relations can help us too. First time job hunters may find it valuable to listen to the advice of their parents or guardians — it likely that they know you better than anyone else!

> Read 1 Thessalonians 5:12,13 and consider how we
> should respond to those who are over us in the Lord.

It may be possible for you to find someone whom you respect and trust to help you review your job. That person need not necessarily be a Christian. It may be someone with greater experience within your profession.

GOD'S SENSE

> Read Psalm 23:2 and Isaiah 49:10 which tell us
> where we can expect God to lead us as we seek Him
> for the right employment.

If you are struggling with the answers from these Scriptures, you may be in the wrong job. Sometimes God allows difficulties. Their purpose is to make us lean on God and not on our own understanding (Prov. 3:5). Although we accept that Christians may be called to suffer in their workplace, we must not necessarily apply this principle to our present circumstances and assume that we will just have to put up with what is going on. If we do not seek God regarding the reason for our suffering, we are in danger of becoming passive about our job and active at blaming God for failing to change things. A recipe for belief in the sacred/secular divide!

Too often, we misinterpret such Scriptures as Mark 8:34 where we are told to deny ourselves and take up our cross. What we deny is our old fleshly life, not our new God-given and God-blessed one. Nowhere are we taught that God is a skinflint, out to make our lives a misery. He calls us His sons and daughters. Certainly the Father disciplines His children, but His heart is to bless them too. He does not say that He will bless us only for a couple of hours on Sundays and ignore the rest of our lives. He wants to bless us during the eighty thousand hours of the forty years that many of us will work. There will be times when we are called to suffer and persevere; there will also be times when we are called to act.

Read Psalm 139 and consider:

Whether we leave God behind when we go to work (w. 7–12).

How many days He has planned for us (v. 16).

How we can measure God's care towards us (w. 17,18).

Read Ephesians 2:10 and note what God has prepared for us.

God has good intentions for our employment. We must use our common sense, seek wisdom from others and pray about the future. Then we can expect clear direction and, even in the tough times, job satisfaction with godly contentment.

Take a moment to review this section. Pray through these questions:

How does my job line up with what I have learned about my own abilities in this chapter?

What areas of my job concern me the most? What areas should I be praying God's blessing into? Am I being called by God to stay in my job despite possible drawbacks?

Should I be considering a change of employment in the light of what I have learned? If so, whom should I go and pray with?

WHAT'S ON OFFER?

A number of different types of employment are described in Scripture. We will split into three main sections (although there are undoubtedly more):

ENVIRONMENTALLY FRIENDLY

The environment is hot news. For the most part, environmental concerns appear to have been hijacked by left wing political groups and 'green' political parties which are often rooted in New Age teachings. I say 'hijacked' because God's people were there first — in response to Scripture. We have already seen from Genesis 2:15 that God wanted man to take care of creation. Other Scriptures show the result of his wickedness:

> How long will the land lie parched and the grass in every field be withered? Because those who live in it are wicked, the animals and birds have perished (Jer. 12:4).

Paul refers to the inevitability of a damaged environment in Romans 8:22 which says:

> We know that the whole creation has been groaning as in the pains of childbirth right up to the present time.

Another reason for the Christian tradition of working in the environment is the new appreciation that God gives us of His work. The created work takes on a new significance when you know the Creator.

> Consider the beautiful poetic description of creation in the first six verses of Psalm 19.

That appreciation is possible for us because of our relationship with God, and is the reason for numbers of God's people working in the environment. They may have a defensive role (e.g. environmental health officer) or a protective one (e.g. the RSPCA or the land and countryside preservation of the National Trust). We are all stewards of God's riches.

BEING NEIGHBOURLY

Many Christians are in the arena of care and education — what we might call the area of service to our neighbours.

Jesus indicates that all of God's teaching revolves around two main commandments:

> Love the Lord your God with all your heart and with all your soul and with all your mind ... Love your neighbour as yourself (Matt. 22:37,39).

Through the ages Christians have responded to the second commandment in service to the community, in teaching children and in the caring professions such as nursing. Today's secular history books tend to forget that in Britain it was Christians who founded schools and hospitals. Passages of Scripture such as Matthew 25:34–40 and 1 Peter 4:7–11 have inspired many servants of God to give their lives in service to the poor and needy, the children and the sick and dying.

USING OUR TALENTS

Read Matthew 25:14–30 and consider:

How the servants who made five and two talents achieved this (v. 16).

What the servant with one talent should have done with it as a minimum (v. 27).

We must break out of the belief that Christians must be involved in caring or teaching to have God's approval. Jesus was quite happy with things like making money, putting it on deposit and gaining interest. Doctors do not earn more of God's blessing than business men and women. Teachers do not have a higher calling than stockbrokers, refuse collectors or computer programmers. Carpentry isn't exactly environmentally friendly, but Jesus did it. Fishing can't be described as a caring profession but Peter did it. Doug Sherman and William Hendricks sum it up well:

> Our teaching generally exalts the soul and neglects the body. As a consequence, I find that we subtly rate careers by the extent to which they contribute to the soul. Careers in ministry come first ... then come careers in the 'helping professions' — counsellors in psychology and psychiatry, doctors ... teachers, nurses, social workers, perhaps mothers ... The third group are the labourers and also the people whose primary goal (supposedly) is to make money ... The money people are the bankers, stockbrokers, real estate developers and entrepreneurs who traffic in all that green stuff — and we know how evil that can be![3]

Whatever our profession, it is God's gift. As we honour our Heavenly Employer in our work we will be satisfied.

WHEN TO CHANGE JOBS

So far, we have studied how to choose a job and what jobs are on offer. If we think that we need to change our job, there are three or four points that I think are worth making:

THE EXCEPTION

Changing jobs should be the exception, not the rule and a career change should not be taken lightly. The steps set out above need to be followed through as a minimum requirement. Scripture backs this up.

When we first become Christians, should we assume that because our life has changed we should also change our job? Consider the recurring phrase in the following verses:

> Nevertheless, each one should retain the place in life that the Lord assigned to him and to which God has called him ... Each one should remain in the situation which he was in when God called him ... Brothers, each man, as responsible to God, should remain in the situation God called him to (1 Cor. 7:17,20,24).

WATCH THE EMOTIONS

Some of us may think that we need a change of direction. Most of us are likely to stay in our chosen profession and move between companies within the area of our expertise. Too many changes are caused by over emotional reactions to a pressured situation, whether that pressure is brought on by boredom, overwork or other factors such as an unreasonable boss. If we keep our emotions in check and do not overreact, we will be able to pray through the situation, talk to others and review the job in the cold light of day. It is a wise principle never to make life changing decisions when emotions are high.

Longer term emotional changes also need to be watched. Some have to deal with mid-life transition.

TAKE IT IN STEPS

> Note what Proverbs 16:9 indicates we should be
> aware of and what Proverbs 19:2 warns us against.

It is always best to take things a step at a time. Re-evaluate your reason for moving. Determine whether it is worth re-negotiating with your current employer. Review alternative careers. Refer to Christians already employed in those areas which interest you. Respond to what you have learned and what God has said to you. Prepare a career resumé and resolve to do something about it!

A friend of ours called Kevin has recently followed through these steps. For a number of years, he had worked as a language teacher but was finding his job increasingly stressful and less and less rewarding. He talked and prayed with others, in order to re-evaluate his reasons for wanting to leave the post. There was certainly no room to re-negotiate at the school. There were no other suitable positions and it appeared that it was not the school but the job which needed reviewing. So he stepped out of teaching altogether and took a job as a barman at Gatwick airport.

Kevin found that being out of the job was the only way that he could take stock of his situation. He had often considered an alternative career in computer programming so now was the time to test that idea. He enrolled on a night school course in programming and referred to Christians in both the programming and teaching professions. After a while, he began to realise how much he was missing the classroom. He prayed a great deal about it and eventually resolved to return to teaching. God confirmed every step and he approached the new teaching post, which was just as challenging as the last, with renewed vision and purpose.

MOVING FOR THE KINGDOM

Have you ever considered changing jobs for the sake of God's Kingdom?

Too often, Christians change jobs because the company asks it of them. They may end up in another part of the country with no friends, no church and no vision. Our Heavenly Employer is at work in the world through His church. We are a part of that church, which will include a commitment to a local body of believers. When a job change involves a geographical move, we must make sure that there is a local church in the place where we are moving to which holds the same beliefs and values as ours. If there is not, either God is calling us to help plant one or He does not want us to move!

Taking this a step further, I believe that God is calling many of us to take career risks for the sake of the Kingdom. Radical Christians need to be planting radical churches. As you hear of church planting initiatives, consider whether you should be involved. If so, start applying for jobs in the area and see what God does!

Note the promises in Psalm 16:11.

In whatever way God moves us on, our new employment is unlikely to resemble the first paragraph in this chapter. Rather, it will probably be a workplace of pressures and personal ambitions which we will need to negotiate to the glory of God.

---

[1] *New American Standard Bible,* The Lockman Foundation (1973).

[2] David J. Frahm, *The Great Niche Hunt,* Navpress (1991), p.42. Used with permission.

[3] Doug Sherman & William Hendricks, *Your Work Matters to God,* Navpress (1987), pp.47–48. Used with permission.

Chapter Four

HOW BIG ARE MY DREAMS?

He was thrown in a pit and left dead for it. He served as a slave for it. He languished in a prison because of it. But he never let go of it. Joseph had a dream. It changed his life. Even in the most terrible circumstances, he held on to what God had told him until the day it was fulfilled. The dream turned out even bigger than Joseph could have imagined. Not only did his family bow down to him, the whole of Egypt acknowledged his greatness (see Genesis chapters 37 to 47). God's dreams are bigger than ours.

We all have dreams — dreams of serving God, of seeing people saved through our witness. We can have dreams for our daily work too. We can ask God either to renew these dreams or give us for the first time ambitions for our employment. Ambition is not something dirty or worldly. Godly ambition is glorious, liberating and also painful and tested. As we begin to dream God's dreams for our job, we can begin to enjoy God's blessing on our work.

WRONG AMBITIONS?

Gerald Coates tells the story of a man who came to see him[1]. He was immaculately dressed, had a smart car and a beautiful house. He was ambitious too — and highly successful according to the world's standards. The tragedy was that he had once aspired to be something for God and now, thirty years on, although materially on top, he was spiritually desolate. At one o'clock in the morning he was kneeling on the floor in Gerald's living room with tears streaming down his face. Fortunately, it was not too late for him to change. But it is better to get the foundations right in the first place.

FOUNDATIONS

The desire to get to the top is one of the deepest drives in human nature. But God wants us to overcome our selfish desires and replace them with His. We must not be caught up with wrong ambitions for reasons of pride, insecurity or material benefit. Rather, we must be ambitious for God. As we seek His kingdom first, everything else will be added (Luke 12:31).

Paul indicates very different ambitions from those we associate with the world.

> Look up 1 Thessalonians 4:11,12 and consider what they are.

DIRECTIONS

Maybe you have ambitions to set up a business for God or to make money for Him. Before you set out on a course of action, make sure that you really have heard from Him on it. He is not interested in religious acts. Some will receive this kind of calling, but many have stepped out on a presumption, as a result of poor teaching or simply out of a desire to 'do something for God'. Where the calling is not clear, the venture is unlikely to succeed.

Our motives must be clear and we must understand that God will probably not reveal to us everything that He has planned. If we think that we know all that God has for us, we may find ourselves running too strongly in the wrong direction or, worse still, stopping short of the finishing tape. As we have already seen, God's dreams are bigger than ours. Oswald Chambers explains it like this:

> In our natural life our ambitions are our own. In the Christian life we have no aim of our own, and God's aim looks like missing the mark because we are too short sighted to see what He is aiming at.[2]

Read James 4:13–15 and consider what wrong assumptions the businessmen are making.

What should all our actions be subject to?

Getting There

Apart from trusting God and seeking His will, is there anything we should be doing to fulfil His dreams? Our Puritan forefathers certainly thought so. They spoke against the sacred/secular divide and argued that there was virtue in our day to day work. In particular, diligence was praised and idleness condemned. They would encourage us to prepare in order to give our best to God in our work. We set our aim as God's aim, and ensure that we do not miss the mark.

QUALIFICATIONS

Qualifications prove that we have both brain power and staying power. In the early years of employment when we are not too experienced, our list of examination results may be what opens or closes the door. If, like me, you didn't pay too much attention to examinations at school, you may need to consider some form of further education. A full-time college course is the best way to obtain a qualification, but if this is not possible, then night school or a correspondence course may be the alternative route.

It is never too late to study. But whenever we consider further education, there are always a hundred and one reasons why now is not a good time. But if you believe that you have been called to serve God to the best of your ability, your abilities may need proving in the examination hall. To set your aim as God's aim may need considerable determination!

Read James 1:12 and consider what you are called to do.

INTERVIEWS

The experts tell us that an interview focuses 60 per cent on how we look and only 40 per cent on what we say! Whether this is true or not, the principle is clear: Dress smartly and smell sweet!

How else can we prepare for an interview? Obviously we must ask God to go before us, to keep the enemy away and to grant us the job if it's the right one. We can also learn as much as possible about the company and, as appropriate, mention what we have learned as the interview progresses. By doing that, we will create the impression that we want the job.

Should we speak about our faith? Yes — provided we are careful not to present it in an aggressive manner. Certainly, we must not be tempted to hide our beliefs during an interview. If we honour God, He will honour us whether we get the job or not.

A friend of mine recently went for a job. When she was asked what her faith meant to her, she answered and then turned the question around and explained what it would mean to her employer. She said that because of her faith, she would work hard, be honest, refuse to gossip, keep to her hours and so on. A good employer will be impressed with such a response.

> Those who honour me I will honour (1 Sam. 2:30).

CLIMBING THE LADDER

We have already seen that God wants to bless us. The most common outworking of this in our employment will be through promotion. We may not see ourselves as different from any other employee but our Christian commitment to our work will be evident to the observant employer.

ALWAYS SAY 'YES'?

Should we always say 'yes' to promotion? We have already looked at the area of moving for the sake of God's Kingdom. But if God is calling us to stay in our local church and the promotion is calling us to go, we must do as God says.

There are other occasions when it may be right to say 'no' to promotion. Kate is a young woman in our church who enjoys her job as a pharmacist at the local hospital. She worked hard at her studies and is well qualified. She works hard now and is widely respected at work. Naturally, her boss is keen for her to progress in her career and there is an accepted promotional route within the profession. Kate, however knows that God has put her where she is and she is happy. So if she were offered promotion, she would not take it.

A refusal of promotion is hard for an employer to understand. His world is likely to revolve around such issues as job identity and status. (Have you ever noticed how often people ask the status assessing question, 'What do you do for a living?') When someone comes along who has identity and status in Someone else, it is not surprising that the boss doesn't understand. In some cases, that lack of understanding may mean our losing the job. Alternatively, it may result in an opportunity to share about Jesus.

Do you have a wrong view of promotion? If so, how does this express itself in your work? (e.g. 'I need the money', 'I'll be able to deal with that person'...)

Pray through these questions:

How sure are you that your status and identity are primarily in Christ? (2 Cor. 5:17)

If God told you to refuse a promotion, how ready would you be to obey?

WHEN WE'VE SAID 'YES'

In most circumstances, promotion reflects the blessing of God on our lives. It is likely to involve greater responsibility which is often expressed in management responsibilities for others. As we progress up the ladder, we will be able to influence the employment pressures of those we manage.

Workplaces suffer from increasing de-personalisation. Whereas the management responsibility of looking after the welfare of employees was once referred to as 'Personnel,' it is now called, 'Human Resources Function'. People are not so much concerned about employee welfare as their usefulness as company resources — along with plant and equipment, finance and technology. Sadly, many managers overlook that fact that without people there would be no organisation. How did the company start? Someone had an idea. How were the profits realised? Someone had the flair and ability to identify the demand and produce the goods. People are a company's most valuable resource and as Christians in management, we can demonstrate this in the way that we treat our employees.

> According to Philippians 2:4–7, what should the attitude of Christians (including Christian managers) be? How might this show itself in practice?

> According to Colossians 4:1, what should managers provide for their employees?

The abolition of the slave trade and the introduction of reasonable working hours have not removed human exploitation and alienation. Where an employer does not have godly motives, he will exploit his employees to varying degrees.

Colossians 3:5–10 sets out eleven ungodly models of behaviour which could be applied to the way an employer might treat his employees. Six of these are impurity, evil desires, greed, rage, malice and lies.

> What are the other five?

In Colossians 3:12–14 we see a further eight models of behaviour which we could attribute to a Christian employer. Four of them are compassion, gentleness, bearing with others and love.

What are the other four?

Whereas performance or expediency may typify the values of today's manager, the Christian in management can set Christ's example of service. He can encourage his employees; build a team; work with them; trust them; delegate jobs and recognise their abilities. A relationship of trust, with wise use of authority, will bring the best out of an employee and, in turn, benefit the company.

It is not possible in a book of this size to do more than touch on management attitudes to employees. For a more detailed analysis, I recommend *Management: A Biblical Approach* by Myron Rush (Victor Books).

If you are in management, consider ways in which you can build an effective team. Think about those who work for you. How can you bring the best out of them? What areas can you delegate to them? How can you encourage them?

DREAM ON

Do you believe God has ambitions for you in your employment? Are you ready to ask Him to expand your area of influence at work? Will you pray for God-given promotion in order to set God's principles of management in place? Are you ready to serve your fellow employees in a management capacity? If so, dream and pray on!

We need to 'work on' too. Our employment is not about putting in the hours while we wait for our real mission from God to begin. If we have God-given ambitions for promotion, we must understand that God has called us to our present employment. We must work hard and be clear about God's goals. Work activities will need as much prayer as church activities.

GOALS AND ACTIONS

Our dreams will remain dreams unless they are backed up with prayer, godly ambition and action. When God gives us a goal, we need to pray, plan and act.

The following may help you devise a plan of action to suit your circumstances:

Vision
Develop a vision of how you would like your job to be. What would you like to achieve in your present job? Where would you like to be in five years' time?

e.g.: I am currently a warehouseman. I would like to categorise the products in a new way to ensure better storage use. In five years I would like to have reached the position of Warehouse Foreman. That is two promotional steps away.

View
Take a view of your job as it stands now. What is the job's purpose? What is the end product of what you do?

e.g.: The main purpose of my job is to see that products are correctly stored and labelled and to move them, as instructed, to other sites. The end product is to ensure that stock availability meets sales requests.

Variance
In what areas is your present situation at variance with the vision you have for your job?

e.g.: I am not given the responsibilities I seek. I have a plan for re-categorising the stock which I believe would improve efficiency. No one is interested in the plan.

Viability
Where the present situation is out of line with the vision, is a change realistic? What steps can be taken to accomplish that change? How much does the change depend on you (new approach to your work, further qualifications, etc.)? How much does it depend on your employer?

e.g.: One of the reasons no one is interested in my proposals is the fact that I have been afraid to air them! I am not sure what people will think of me if I start suggesting changes. I know my identity is in Christ and not in the way others think of me and I am sure my plan is good. I will discuss the changes with my boss at the first opportunity and will leave his reaction with God. At least I can pray about my boss's response! Working with management in such a way may be the first step to realising my godly ambition of being the Warehouse Foreman.

A STEP AT A TIME

If you are serious about serving God's purposes at work, you must have a plan of action.

I would encourage you to write it out, perhaps using the above headings. Pray as you go and be careful to take only one step at a time. Check out your thoughts with others and trust that God will confirm your plans or redirect you. We must always be prepared to be wrong or, more likely, only partially right.

Proverbs 16:9 says:

> In his heart a man plans his course, but the LORD
> determines his steps.

Trust God that this will happen for you.

GIANTS IN THE LAND

'There are some good ideas here, maybe I'll look at them tomorrow.'

'It's all very well in theory but you don't know my boss/company/circumstances.' (Delete as appropriate!)

'I'm not sure where this will take me. Am I ready for this kind of commitment?'

The three most common giants that will prevent us seeing the realisation of our dreams are these: fear of others, fear of the unknown and a lack of commitment. Will we be like the majority of the Israelites as they stood on the borders of Canaan, or will we be like Joshua and Caleb? They saw the giants but they also saw their God. They remembered what He had done for them and were not willing to allow a few giants to get in the way of His purposes.

Read Numbers 13:30; 14:8 and consider Caleb's
proviso for going up and taking the land.

Will you be like Joseph and hold on to your dreams whatever the circumstances? It is time Christians took their work seriously. God's dreams for your employment are bigger than yours. And He wants you to start dreaming.

I will let Charles Swindoll sum up:

> People who soar like eagles, people who live above the drag of the mediocre, are people of dreams. They have God-given drive because they have received God-given dreams ... What are your dreams for this year? What are your hopes, your agenda? What are you trusting God for?[3]

---

[1] Gerald Coates, *Fulness Magazine*, Volume 27. Used with permission.

[2] Oswald Chambers, *Living Water*, Marshall Pickering (1987), p.8. Used with permission.

[3] Charles R. Swindoll, *Living Above the Level of Mediocrity*, Word Books (1987), p.98. Used with permission.

Chapter Five

WHEN THE WORLD PRESSES IN

If the day had started at 9.00 a.m. then Samantha might have been smiling. As it was, it had begun at 7.00 a.m. with the realisation that the refuse collectors were due to come. All the rubbish at the back of the house had to be moved to the front before she left for work — and it was raining. On top of that, young Gary was complaining of a sore throat; there wasn't been time to take the dog out; the library books were overdue (again), and Samantha's husband was away until Saturday. What right did her boss have to ask her to work late in view of this mounting personal crisis?!

We live in a world where today's patients at the doctor's surgery are just as likely to be renewing their subscription for tranquillisers as they are for cough medicine. Today's illnesses are ulcers, nervous breakdowns, blood pressure and hypertension. To survive a day with only a few expletives and a mild headache is a triumph for many in the workplace.

THE WHOLE PICTURE

The pace of life today almost numbs our senses. Work is only one element which threatens to overtake and swallow us up as we valiantly fight to keep our heads above water. In this chapter, we will be concentrating on pressures in the workplace, but because every area of our lives is interconnected, let's look first at the whole picture.

Set out below is an example of a simple time chart. Copy the chart on a larger sheet of paper and write on it your major activities through each hour of each day. It may take some time but should prove worthwhile. The spaces allow only a brief description and some suggested headings might be: Work, TV, Reading, Sports, Meal, Hobby, Leisure, Social, Study, Church, Quiet Time, Family, etc.

For the sake of space, normal working hours have been reduced to one box, covering three or four hours. If you are a shift/night worker, you will need to adjust the hours accordingly.

	Monday	Tuesday	Wednesday	Thursday	Friday	Saturday	Sunday
7.00 — 8.00							
8.00 — 9.00							
9.00 — 1.00							
1.00 — 2.00							
2.00 — 5.00							
5.00 — 6.00							
6.00 — 7.00							
7.00 — 8.00							
8.00 — 9.00							
9.00 — 10.00							
10.00 — 11.00							

Having completed the table, write down the approximate number of hours taken up by each activity, through the week.

ACTIVITY	HOURS	ACTIVITY	HOURS
Work	_____	TV	_____
Reading	_____	Sports	_____
Meals	_____	Leisure	_____
Hobby	_____	Social	_____
Study	_____	Church	_____
Quiet Time	_____	Family	_____
Other	_____	Other	_____
Other	_____	Other	_____

Now put a number by each activity according to the number of hours spent on it (i.e. the number one activity will have the most hours spent on it, number two the second most, etc.).

Note the number order. Has the exercise turned out as you expected? Is it as you think it should be?

Note the importance of work in terms of hours. Can we really afford to relegate it?

How many hours are in the TV column, compared to church or devotional activities?

For many of us, TV can be the soothing influence after a hard day, but should it be?

Ignoring work, what would you change? Go through the hours set against each activity, and adjust them to what you would prefer them to be. Then, using a different coloured pen, go through the time chart and adjust the activities accordingly. Be realistic, not super-spiritual. Don't try and cut out all the leisure activities in favour of Bible studies and Quiet Times. Once you feel that you have a good balance of activities, pray them through. Talk to your partner if you are married; to your house group leaders if you are not. See how realistic they think you have been.

If we have a strong relationship with God coupled with a good balance of healthy leisure activities, we will reduce the stress on our lives. We will then pray through the activities of the day, receive God's help for them and be in full control of what happens.

The balance of leisure activities to work will have great effect on our lifestyles. Leland Ryken's book *Work and Leisure in Christian Perspective* (IVP) is helpful in taking us on through some of the principles outlined above.

CRISIS IN THE WORKPLACE

A crisis in the workplace will often be a reflection of a crisis in other areas of our lives. An imbalance between work and leisure will, in itself, create a pressure.

Christians have an answer to crisis. When Christ died on the cross, He dealt with the ultimate crisis. He knows about life's problems and has overcome them. So what major crises are we likely to face in our work?

NINE TO FIVE?

Many people put in far more hours than the standard 'nine to five'. Their job may be the type for which standard hours do not apply. Or, if they run their own business, it may be difficult to separate work from other daily activities. For many, though, work has become an addictive drug. It consumes them; they cannot stop thinking about it; they even worship it. Here are some of the reasons for developing into a workaholic:

A wrong view of work — it becomes an idol, more important than all else.

A wrong view of self — the satisfaction of personal needs becomes the focal point of life.

A driven character — you have to be the best. If someone has wounded you, you feel that you now have a point to prove.

A wrong view of success — confusing wealth with happiness.

A desperate desire to be liked — shown through achievement for the boss or company.

The desire to be seen as successful — the designer label image.

An escape from the pressures of family life — a preference for the area where you appear to be a success, rather than the family who know what you are really like.

Check that you have not been affected by the world's views of success.

Read through the list again, prayerfully asking God to point out any areas where you may have been affected.

> According to Psalm 115:4–8, what is the end result for those who put their trust in idols?

> According to 1 Corinthians 15:10, what is the secret to working hard without being a workaholic?

If self worth is equated with career success, the effect of business failure can be devastating. Numerous books tell us how to be successful, how to be self fulfilled and meet our personal needs. The self made person is glamorised, but he builds his life on shaky foundations. The cost of his success is stress and unhappiness. Ill health and burnout. So let's be aware of the pressures on our lives in this area.

IT'S ONLY MONEY?

'It's only money'. I used to sing that song as a teenager. We may sing it, but few of us can say, 'I'm not the least bit bothered whether I've got money or not.' Our attitude towards money and possessions is important. We are in trouble when we make a god of our pay, confuse money with happiness and assume that the highest paid jobs are the best. If our attitude to money is wrong, our attitude to work will also be wrong and we will become stressed.

Someone once challenged the Argentine evangelist Omar Cabrera on the subject of possessions. 'Since you are such a successful preacher,' he said, 'with such magnificent offerings from your meetings, you must have a very nice house.' Cabrera replied that he was still living in the same small house today as when he got married. Then he added that he was not interested in bricks and mortar down here. He was more concerned that as people were saved, he was throwing bricks up to heaven where God was preparing a mansion for him!

Writing to the Philippians, Paul says:

> I have learned to be content whatever the circumstances. I know what it is to be in need, and I know what it is to have plenty. I have learned the secret of being content in any and every situation, whether well fed or hungry, whether living in plenty or in want. I can do everything through him who gives me strength (Phil. 4:11–13).

How does Paul's secret apply to your situation? Carefully consider any specific financial areas that you need to pray through.

We should note that it is not money which is evil, but the love of money (1 Tim. 6:10). Someone in our church admitted that she felt uneasy about having money so that as soon as she had any, she spent it! The consequence was debt. Church leaders need to be clear in their teaching on money — both in the context of preaching and in one to one counselling. People in the workplace are unlikely to hear teaching on saving, tithing and giving to the poor.

WAITING FOR TEA BREAKS?

If overwork and a wrong view of money cause stress, so does a lack of work. The tea break may not be so prevalent in workplaces today, but the tea break mentality still manifests itself. There really is some truth in the statement: if you want a job doing quickly, you give it to the busiest person you can find! Living for the weekend can never be a right approach to our work, however mundane that work may seem. A lazy attitude will eventually result in stress — because we are not following the Maker's instructions. The theologian, John Calvin, summarised the problem as follows:

> It will be no slight relief from cares, labours, troubles, and other burdens for a man to know that God is his guide in all these things ... No task will be so sordid and base, provided you obey your calling in it, that it will not shine and be reckoned very precious in God's sight.[1]

If your motives are right and things still do not improve, it may be time to consider whether you are in the right job.

Read 2 Thessalonians 3:6–15 and consider why idleness is frowned upon.

What is Paul's model?

Read Proverbs 13:4 and consider who are the fully satisfied.

SECOND CLASS CITIZENS?

Redundancy, unemployment and lack of qualifications — those who have suffered in any of these areas will relate to the title of this section. A friend who was out of work through no fault of his own, admitted to me that just being out of work for four weeks made him feel incredibly guilty.

If too much work damages people, so does too little work — because work is God ordained. There is a legitimate pride and dignity in it. If we do not work for long periods of time, we are likely to lose our sense of self esteem. We will then stop seeing ourselves as God sees us, lose our vision for our work and have no desire to find another job. If God wants the best for us, then we need to face redundancy as a test and not accept it as a permanent state.

Naturally, we are not meant to use self effort to get ourselves sorted out, nor are we meant to race around in a blind panic trying to find something suitable. God wants to comfort and encourage us. He is the shelter from the storm (Ps. 61:4), our strength in scaling the walls of unemployment and redundancy (2 Sam. 22:30) and the answer when the world presses in.

Pray for someone you know who is unemployed and remember to encourage them when you next see them.

If people who reach retirement do not understand how God sees them, they may begin to feel worthless. But just as God prepared our job, so He has prepared our retirement. It is really retirement with a small 'r' since we can never retire from serving God, nor would we want to. But we can prepare ourselves for retirement from work by seeing that we have an adequate pension, by enrolling on pre-retirement courses and by remaining active.

If we have a strong relationship with God, we will be able to meet the challenges of unemployment, redundancy and retirement in Him.

Lack of qualifications has already been discussed but it is worth noting that not everyone will be called by God to seek further examination passes. God is not primarily interested in our intellect.

> Read Psalm 51:17 and consider what qualifications
> He looks for.

Throughout history God has chosen the seemingly poorly qualified to fulfil His purposes. Fishermen and tax collectors turned the world upside down. Both William Carey, the first missionary to India, and D. L. Moody, the famous American evangelist, started life in the shoe trade. God's qualifications are not ours. We look on the outward; He looks on the heart. So let's not be pressed in by the world in the area of promotion or educational success. There are no second class citizens in God's Kingdom.

---

[1] John Calvin, *Institutes of the Christian Religion*, Book III, Chapter X, para 6. Westminster Press edition, edited by John T. McNeill, p.724.

Chapter Six

A WOMAN'S WORLD?

I feel particularly unqualified to write this chapter. The main problem is that I'm a man. (My wife tells me that's the problem with most men!) I decided to ask Wendy McFee to write for me. Wendy is British but she works as a principal in a consultancy firm in New York. I have asked her to help us understand the particular issues that a woman has to face in the workplace.

Wendy: Before I start, I should like to emphasise that THIS IS NOT THE POINT AT WHICH MEN SHOULD STOP READING and turn to the next chapter. This subject will benefit any Christian man who works with women or comes across women in every day life. Indeed, at least one section of this chapter is equally applicable to men.

EQUAL BUT DIFFERENT

I am not a feminist. I would, however, contend that women are equal to men in God's eyes, but that they are different. If you haven't thought about the basic differences between men and women, then you'll be less likely to understand the unique problems and opportunities that working women face.

A major obstacle to many women becoming Christians is the idea that God regards them as inferior. How can they reconcile such questions as: Why did God require a longer period for a woman to be unclean after the birth of a female child than a male child (Lev. 12)? Why is the first-born male so important (Exod. 34:19–20)? Why does Scripture often appear to speaking only to men (Lev. 18). Why do women seem to be relegated to second place (1 Cor. 11:2–16; Eph. 5:22–33; Col. 3:18–25; 1 Tim. 2:9–15; 1 Pet. 3:1–7)?

Probably the most convincing argument concerning women's supposed inferiority concerns Jesus' relationship with women.

Reflect on the way that Jesus related to the following four women.

Mary (Luke 10:38–42; John 11; 12:1–8).

Martha (Luke 10:38–42; John 11; 12:1–8).

Mary Magdalene (Luke 8:2; John 20:10–18).

The Samaritan woman (John 4:7–26).

Jesus evidently had a lot of interaction with women and regarded them as equal to men. Women often suffer from low self esteem — frequently because of the way that men (often family members) have treated them. Christian women can be set free from this when they realise how much God values them.

IN WHAT WAYS ARE WOMEN DIFFERENT?

A complete list of the ways in which women differ from men is not within the scope of this chapter. Neither would it be relevant. Our focus is on women in the workplace. For a broader look at this subject, see *Honouring Marriage* by John and Liz Wilthew in the *How To* series. So let's look at just four ways in which women differ from men.

WOMEN CAN HAVE CHILDREN!

Obviously women differ from men in that they can have children. If a woman has a child, she has a choice to make — either to stay at home and devote her time to her child(ren) or to find a childminder and continue her career.

Traditionally, Christians argue that nothing can replace a mother's tender-loving care during a child's formative years.

However, some Christian mothers believe that they need the mental stimulation of their occupations and feel that, 'My children would suffer if I had to stay at home all day.'

We are sometimes quick to judge mothers who choose to work. We shouldn't do this (Matt. 7:1), but we should also note that there are no verses which state that mothers should always stay at home and look after their children. Both parents carry the responsibility for their children's welfare. However, since a woman has a natural instinct to do this, it is appropriate for her to stay at home if this is financially possible. Assuming there is a choice, most Christian mothers would choose to do so.

If a mother does return to the workplace, she really has two jobs and is likely to become very tired. Further, if the child is sick, it generally falls to the mother to take time off work to look after him/her. This situation requires an understanding employer. Or it could place the mother at risk of losing her job or not receiving promotion. Thankfully, progressive companies are becoming more aware of the importance of women in the workplace.

Of course, there are occasions when a mother must work simply to survive (e.g. in one parent families or when economic necessity dictates that both parents work. In such cases, there is no choice).

Thomas and Mary live in the black township of Khayelitsha, Cape Town. They have three young children. If both parents do not work, they will not survive. The Vineyard Fellowship in Cape Town recognise this problem and have set up an all day crèche facility in the township. The children can be left in safe hands while both parents work. Another result of the initiative is that friendship between the church and the township has increased and an excellent witness established.

Sometimes the woman is the main or only breadwinner (e.g. because she earns more than her husband or because he cannot find employment or is pursuing further education). Whether the husband should stay at home and look after the children depends on the circumstances, including how adept he would be at childminding.

If a woman decides to stay at home to bring up the children, it is important that her husband esteems and appreciates what she is doing. She may be able to work from home if suitable work can be found — and if she has any energy left! Some Christian women in America are 'homeschooling' their children.

As the children grow older, the mother may be able to return to part-time or full-time work. The opportunity to do this will probably be greater in the traditionally woman-dominated occupations (e.g. nursing, teaching and secretarial). Skills may need to be updated in these areas and also in the practical employment area, encompassing shop floor jobs and those jobs which have close links with technology. If the woman was in middle or senior management when she left, the possibility of her returning to a similar position is small.

> Read Proverbs 31:10–31 and, with particular reference to verses 16–18, consider whether the passage is speaking only of 'housework' or of actual employment.

> With reference to verses 20,21 consider whether the married woman is concerned only for her household.

> How do other people view her because of her work?

SEXUAL DIFFERENCES

Please take a moment now to review what Ralph has already said on this subject in Chapter Two. Christian women need to smile and be friendly, but they have to watch that they're not misinterpreted. In some work environments, men will watch the way women respond to their double entendres so women must be careful how they react.

The way women dress says a lot about them too. As Ralph has already pointed out, the enemy will make this area one of his major targets for men. Christian women must dress and behave appropriately.

Women must be as 'shrewd as snakes and as innocent as doves' (Matt. 10:16). In other words, they must be aware of how easily they can be caught in a relationship with a man — particularly when its beginning seems so innocent. What counts is not just the letter of the law but the spirit of it (Matt. 5:28). If a woman's sexual or emotional needs are met in a fashion that is not godly, she will lose her intimacy with the Lord.

WOMEN ARE MORE EMOTIONAL

Women tend to be more emotional than men. This is usually perceived as a weakness, although they are usually more considerate and caring. They are also more intuitive and often more creative.

Our society encourages competition. Competition between women can lead to jealousy. In a company it's better to encourage team building than competition. Jealousy can then be replaced by trust and harmony and competition can be reserved for external activities. This is easier said than done.

Aside from the negative emotions, men would do well to remember that a woman's emotions can be a positive contribution to the workplace. In applying her whole being to her work, she is committed in a way which men do not always find possible. This commitment and enthusiasm will often greatly benefit the employer.

GOSSIP

The *Oxford Illustrated Dictionary* begins to define 'gossip' as follows:

1. (archaic) Familiar acquaintance; (esp. woman) friend.
2. Idle talker, newsmonger, tattler (esp. of woman).[1]

There is a commonly-held perception that women gossip more than men. In my experience, they gossip as much as each other in the office! This doesn't make it right, of course. Gossip is one of the most difficult issues that the Christian has to face in the workplace. It is so destructive. Ralph touched on this in Chapter Two and I want to expand on it here. I mentioned earlier that there was at least one section which applied equally to men and women. This is it!

> Read through the following verses and note the negative and positive results of gossip: Prov. 11:13; 16:28; 20:19; 26:20.

God wants us to refrain from gossiping. Ephesians 4:29 gives us some guidance on how to do this:

> **Do not let any unwholesome talk come out of your mouths, but only what is helpful for building others up according to their needs, that it may benefit those who listen.**

When others are tearing down the boss (or anyone else for that matter), should you just keep quiet (which could be interpreted as tacit approval) or should you take active steps, like mentioning his/her good points or walking away from the conversation? Pray quietly on the spot and God will guide you.

We've looked at four ways in which women are or are perceived to be different from men and which have implications for Christian women at work. There are doubtless more.

> Proverbs 11:16 sets out an interesting difference in character between women and men (I hasten to add, not all men!).

> How might the results of the woman's kind-heartedness show in the workplace?

> Note the best quality of all in Proverbs 31:30.

> How might a woman's godliness show itself in the workplace?

THE SINGLE CHRISTIAN WOMAN

In our first 'difference,' we looked at some special considerations for married Christian women. I now want to turn to single Christian women. To some extent, our main focus will be on single women in executive positions (as I am able to write from experience on this issue!). But the principles hold good for single women, whatever the employment.

Society, and sometimes even the church, puts pressure on people to be married. It is however, good to be single (1 Cor. 7:8–9,32).

I think it is acceptable for women to be bosses. The New Testament states that a man should be head over the church (1 Tim. 3:1,2) and that a husband should be head over his wife (Eph. 5:22–33 — although note what the husband has to do in return!). I can't find any Scriptures in the New Testament that indicate that a woman cannot be 'head' in secular life. Nevertheless, society rarely accords the same respect to women as it does to men.

Since most married Christian women have children and leave the workforce (at least for a few years) to bring up their children, any female Christian executives are in general single. By contrast, male Christian executives are usually married. They are supported by their wives (at home) who look after the house, children, etc. The (single) female Christian executive does not have this support.

Even though many companies are making an effort to promote women, the women in many companies have to work much harder for promotion than their male counterparts. In large companies women hold very few positions in senior management. Those that 'make' it have to be assertive and in many instances are much more aggressive than their male counterparts, often to the detriment of their femininity.

The single woman who is not yet at a managerial level does well to remember who her employer really is. She may be frustrated by assumptions that she is not seeking promotion (preferring a future husband and family instead). As ever, she must refer everything to her Heavenly Employer.

The single Christian woman executive has to balance a number of issues. She must try to behave as Jesus would; fit in Christian commitments outside working hours; cope with a (usually) heavy workload; be denied the degree of authority that is accorded to a male counterpart and not have the support that a loving spouse and family provide. Certainly she has the most important Foundation — Jesus is all-sufficient. But she must look to Him in everything or she may idolise work or, in her loneliness, engage in inappropriate or ungodly relationships. Speaking personally, I do not strive for promotion. I know who the Boss is and that I'm already fully accepted by Him.

DO YOU PREFER TO WORK FOR A WOMAN OR A MAN?

It is often said that women prefer to work for men than for women. It is sometimes said that they can manipulate a male boss better than a female boss. Further, women bosses are thought to be more demanding. As Christians, we must not manipulate others. And our work should satisfy demanding people — unless those demands are unreasonable.

Because of male pride, it may be hard for a man to accept a woman as his superior. But in general, I think that most reasonable men will accept and respect a competent woman boss.

DO YOU RESPECT WOMEN?

Take a few moments to examine your heart and conscience. Jesus loves us all equally. He died for everyone, so everyone deserves to be respected.

Think (whether you're a man or a woman) of the women you work with. Are you respectful, compassionate, fair?

If you are having problems with a woman at work (especially, if you're a woman), prayerfully consider opening the lines of communication. It may not be easy but you could win a friend, a valuable team member and, most important of all, advance the Kingdom.

If you're a woman, is there anything in the way you dress or in your behaviour towards men that you should change?

Do you relate to women in the same way Jesus did? Return to the passages we studied at the beginning of this chapter and pray through the observations you have made on the relationship between Jesus and women.

---

[1] *Oxford Illustrated Dictionary*, Oxford University Press (1962, 1975). Used with permission.

Chapter Seven

How to Run a Betting Shop

W ell, you must admit the title got you to read on! Here we are going to look at some of the more contentious and difficult questions raised in relation to our employment. What about Christian businesses? Can I be in a non-Christian partnership? What is the Protestant Work Ethic? Should I join a Union? Should I work on Sunday? Are New Age practices infiltrating the workplace? Is all work legitimate (and how do you run a betting shop)?

Separate from the World?

The argument is that Christians should have nothing to do with non-Christian practices. We are called to be different and show the alternative. But is such thinking strictly true?

Read 2 Corinthians 6:14–18.

This passage is often used in the context of not marrying someone who does not share your beliefs. But in context it has a general meaning, and therefore a general application. So how do we apply the passage? Is it about not working with unbelievers, or not even mixing with them? Where do you draw the line?

What do you think?

If we take the passage too far, we end up in a monastery. If we ignore it altogether, we could find our energy and resources tied into some rather dubious business ventures. Paul wrote the passage for a reason — he was concerned over some of the actions of the Corinthian believers. It may be that his particular concern relates to the false prophets mentioned later (2 Cor. 11:13–14).

Whatever worried Paul, it is a brave Bible expositor who concludes that to 'come out from them' means that we must have dealings only with believers. And it is a foolish expositor who ignores the warning altogether as something only applicable to the situation at the time. Once again, we need to lean on God's sense, other people's sense and our own common sense (see Chapter Three). Other passages of Scripture will also help us to understand a little more about our relationship with unbelievers:

> Read John 15:19;17:11,14–19 which highlights your relationship with the world.

> Read 2 Corinthians 10:3–4 and note against whom or what you are fighting.

> Read Matthew 5:13–14 and consider what Jesus calls us to be like and consider how this might have its effect on the world.

These verses help to shed light on the earlier passage in 2 Corinthians 6. It is worth noting that the passage dealing with the identity of our real enemies is in the same letter that calls us to live separately. Paul was not advocating a monastic existence.

> Look again at Matthew 5:13–14. How can Christians be salt if they are not in the world?

Salt preserves, and by actively participating in the world, we are affecting it, preserving godly values when all around are abandoning them. Jesus also calls us to be light and links that picture to that of a city set on a hill. The city is obviously separate in order to be noticed and shine. So we are called to be both in the world (but not of it) and separate from it (but not cut off from it).

Relating this to the workplace, we could argue that those of us in daily employment tend to be the salt, while those of us working in the church or setting up Christian businesses are the light. Both salt and light are necessary in the establishment of God's Kingdom. Christian businesses and those not run by Christians are equally valid. We are not extra-special Christians if we work in a specifically Christian concern.

Working in a Christian business creates a number of pressures. Your boss is a Christian and will expect you to react in a certain way. If you disagree with him, you are supposed to reason things out peaceably, without a shouting match. If the boss is unwise, he may use the fact that you are a Christian to work you harder than is reasonable, or to pay you less than the market rate (quoting the appropriate passages of Scripture of course!). Hopefully, such examples will be the exception, not the rule. It is thrilling to work together as believers, particularly when the cause is clear and God given.

We are all salt and light, in different proportions, according to our employment.

Non-Christian Partnerships?

Most of us would have no problem applying 2 Corinthians 6:14–18 to marriage, but what about starting a business partnership with someone who does not share your beliefs? This is something of a minefield. I propose taking the coward's way out, describing three of the most common views and leaving it to you to sort out which you feel is appropriate. Here again, we must seek the wise advice of others and maintain our relationship with God.

IT CAN NEVER BE RIGHT

Some people say, 'Scripture is clear: we should not be yoked together with unbelievers — so you must form a partnership with believers, never with unbelievers.' The issue here does not concern working with unbelievers, but setting up in business together. In a partnership, there is usually a financial commitment and a legal agreement, so the stakes are high. Although you may be best friends now, the unbeliever has a different set of values from you and one day this may cause conflict.

IT CAN SOMETIMES BE RIGHT

This argument looks at the circumstances, then it looks at the whole picture. What sort of partnership is it? For example, the larger legal, accountancy and actuarial firms count their partners in tens and twenties, rather than in ones and twos. This arrangement is not so very different from a normal employment contract — even if it does have a financial or legal undertaking. If the partner is one individual — your lifelong best buddy — should you automatically reject all thought of a partnership with him?

IT IS ALMOST ALWAYS RIGHT

Advocates of this view say that with the odd exception any business partnership is fine provided you go into it with your eyes open. The passage of Scripture in 2 Corinthians 6 refers to a joining or 'yoking'. Unlike a marriage which is 'till death do us part', you can always dissolve a business partnership (although the financial cost of doing so may be high). So, if there is no 'yoking', there is no problem. Obviously, the usual prudent business rules apply, but they don't hinge on the term 'partnership'.

As we have already discovered, our work is a partnership firstly with God. As we keep our relationship with Him clear, and seek Him on our every move, we will avoid mistakes and ensure we are in the world but not of it.

> Note the relationship between God's work and our work in partnership, as expressed in Psalm 90:16–17:
>
> **May your deeds be shown to your servants, your splendour to their children. May the favour of the Lord our God rest upon us; establish the**

work of our hands for us — yes, establish the
work of our hands.

What Is the Protestant Work Ethic?

I include this question because although we may not be aware of
it, many of our modern day politicians refer to the Protestant or
Puritan work ethic and apply it to modern day work practices and
attitudes.

First let's have a quick history lesson. From as far back as the
Greeks and Romans, work was viewed as a curse. In Greek society,
you were free if you had no daily toil and were able to devote
yourself to art, philosophy or politics. The Middle Ages introduced
the sacred/secular divide in which work was seen as a poor second
rate existence as compared to Holy Orders. It was against this
background that Reformation leaders such as Luther and Calvin,
together with the English and Scottish Puritans, brought such
welcome biblical teaching. Naturally, they touched on more than
just a Scriptural work ethic — although practical daily work began
to reflect much of what was taught.

The central pillar of a majority of this teaching was an understanding of the sovereignty of God. He was seen as sovereign over
all of life, so man's labour had both been created by Him and
mattered to Him. Work therefore gained a dignity which had been
sadly lacking in the earlier ages.

Inevitably, this healthy attitude to work brought its reward in
successful businesses, prosperity and contentment. The idle were
condemned and the diligent approved — although the poor were
not forgotten and social care was part and parcel of the teaching.

Scriptures such as Ecclesiastes 9:10 were often quoted:

Whatever your hand finds to do, do it with all
your might.

One of the more colourful quotes from Martin Luther goes as follows:

> God does not want success to come without work ... He does not want me to sit at home, to loaf, to commit matters to God, and to wait till a fried chicken flies into my mouth. That would be tempting God.[1]

The teaching was based on a relationship with God. Without this anchor, it was open to abuse in the workplace.

In late twentieth-century Britain, the pursuit of excellence has become a God which is expressed in terms of material success and hard work. Without God at the centre, the work ethic becomes a dangerous and misused tool. The politically astute have manipulated the truth and have done great damage to what was once a Scriptural concept of work. The pursuit of riches and the 'looking after number one' philosophy are pinned to the Puritans and are wrongly assumed to have God's seal of approval. So beware when you hear mention of the Protestant or Puritan work ethic today. What is being described may have little relationship to what was actually taught by the original Reformers and Puritans.

SHOULD I JOIN A UNION?

Unions have often been seen as synonymous with picket line violence and left wing political manipulation. But they have not always had this reputation. Trade Unions were legally recognised in the UK for the first time in the 1820s and at their forefront were many notable Christians. Indeed, the main reasons for the rise of the Trade Union movement had to do with protection against exploitive employers, unsafe working practices, child labour and other worker abuses. Many of the early unions were based on godly principles. Sadly, these have disappeared over the years.

In their place, the unions introduced the more questionable practices of securing higher rates of pay, lower numbers of hours and political gain. And should negotiations with management fail, the threat of strikes always hung in the air. Although the 'closed shop' of required union membership is a thing of the past, many Christians still struggle with the concept of union membership because of former practices.

> Consider the emphasis of the following verses: Luke 3:14; 1 Timothy 6:6; Hebrews 13:5.
>
> In what way do you think these emphases might be seen as opposing membership of a Trade Union?

If we simply conclude from these verses that union membership can never be right for a Christian, we are viewing only half the story. The other half has already been discussed in earlier chapters. The employer can never be 'whiter than white'. Abuses and exploitation still exist — although in more 'acceptable' forms. There is an over-emphases on profit margins, and often a consequent lack of respect for the worker. So the union can act as a very useful conscience for the over enthusiastic boss.

Perhaps the question to ask is not 'should I join a union?' but 'where are the Christians in the unions?' Many Christians who treat work as a necessary evil have assumed that unions too are evil and have refused to be involved in them.

Consider what qualities and concerns a Christian trade unionist would bring to the negotiating table.

Should I Work on a Sunday?

Central to the dramatic story depicted in *Chariots of Fire* was Eric Liddell's refusal to run in the Olympics on a Sunday. In 1991,

Jonathan Edwards, the UK's leading triple jumper dropped out of both the World Athletic Championships and the Europa Cup Finals for the same reason. In that same year, many of the UK's leading supermarket chains deliberately broke the law by opening on Sundays close to Christmas, and challenged the law by declaring that they intended to continue the practice. Working on Sunday is still a hot issue!

Should Christians refuse to work on Sundays? What if we have jobs for which Sunday working is normal? If we argue that a shop worker should not work, what about a nurse or a fireman?

> Read Matthew 12:1–14 and note Jesus' attitude to the Sabbath.

> What do you feel about Sunday working?

The creation story speaks of a day of rest. Those who are on shifts and have to work on Sundays must have a day of rest for the sake of their health. If an employer is operating within the law, he will ensure this anyway. Those with second jobs (unless both are part-time) are steadily moving towards a breakdown.

In what is no longer a Christian country, it is difficult to go against the tide. If our job gives the option of not working on Sunday, let's take it — and explain the reason to our boss. In some cases we will risk disapproval — but our ultimate employer is heavenly. If our job really is at risk — and we know that we are in the right place — we may have to accept an employer's request to work on occasional Sundays.

Let's applaud people like Jonathan Edwards, but recognise that he stood up for what he believed God was saying to him at the time. Having a day of rest helps stop the greedy supermarkets and blesses the workaholic employee. But imposed regulations will not motivate us to set aside a day which is holy to God (Exod. 20:8–10). Only a change of heart will do that.

IS NEW AGE INFILTRATING THE WORKPLACE?

Not all managers undervalue their staff and overvalue the profit margins. A number of employers hold their workforce in high esteem, whether for the sake of maximising results or for more compassionate motives. The tragedy is that with the demise of Christian practices in the workplace, the methods of employee care and promotion have become increasingly secular.

Alongside the employee training and educational programmes, there is often a good dose of what have come to be known as New Age practices. These are wide ranging in their content. For a broad statistical look at New Age influence in this country, I recommend Marc Europe's *Monograph 35: The New Age is Coming*!

Educational and personal development programmes in the modern company may encompass such matters as 'Releasing and Realising Your Potential', 'Visualisation and Goal Setting', or 'Increasing Your Performance Level'. These titles seem innocent enough but they mask the real teaching of the course which will often include meditation techniques learned from the Hindu religion, or from Transcendental Meditation as expounded by the Guru Maharishi Mahesh Yogi. Eastern philosophies, suitably westernised (e.g. 'Self Talk' or 'Breakthrough') are increasingly taught on business courses. These techniques enable the employee to reach states of consciousness beyond his rational mind. Hypnosis is not uncommonly practised. It is often linked to projecting the employee out of his body and encouraging him to commune with 'imaginary' counsellors.

New Age teaching in the business world is much more common in the States than in the UK. But what is in the States today usually reaches the UK tomorrow. Already, a number of larger British companies are looking into this area and (often innocently) introducing some of the techniques into their training courses.

> Note what Romans 1:21–23,25 teaches us about this increasing influence.

Note how 2 Thessalonians 2:15 applies to us as we face these increasing influences.

Are there any New Age influences in your company training courses?

Pray and seek advice before approaching anyone within the company regarding the course content.

IS ALL WORK LEGITIMATE?

We have already noted that work is God's gift and have also touched on the curse introduced by Adam. Satan wants to see the continued corruption of all that is good and reflects the work of God. So he twists what is good (sex, work) and turns it into something evil in which believers can play no part. There is no need for me to emphasise the illegality of working as a drug pusher, a thief or a prostitute. But what about the person who works for an armaments factory, a cigarette company, a bar or a betting shop (to come back to the title of this chapter)?

Every generation faces these grey areas and Christians are likely to give more than one response. What is acceptable to one may not be so to another (1 Cor. 8:7–9). Martin Luther spoke of three vocations that were not open to the Christian; prostitution, the priesthood and banking! So watch it, all you budding bank managers!

The grey areas change and we must seek God and others about our response. We must be careful not to judge a job on what may, on investigation, represent 'indirect evil'. For example: refusing to work at the local council offices because a majority of the councillors agree with abortion, or deciding not to work for a film company because they once produced a particularly violent film. We are not likely to find a job which does not in some way have an indirectly evil side to it.

There are a couple of further points worth making. Firstly, we should not judge worthy vocations on the basis of utility value. A company which produces fire alarms must not be judged as a better company than one which sells oil paintings. We may think that fire alarms are more useful, but we have a creative God and paintings and music are also God's gifts to us.

Secondly, there may be jobs which can never be described as evil but which may not be as useful to society as others. I have always wondered how much job satisfaction there is for the person who makes the paper umbrellas for cocktail drinks! Again, there are various shades of grey here and I am in danger of arguing against myself on the matter of utility value. There will always be a positive element in most jobs. It's just that if you can work for the more useful jobs to society, so much the better.

Are there any areas in your job which might be out of bounds for the Christian?

Are there any areas in your company where there is 'indirect evil'? What should you be praying for here?

In what areas can you see your job serving others, however indirectly (e.g. It earns you money to care for others)?

We haven't answered the question posed by the chapter heading yet. How does a Christian run a betting shop? He closes down all bets except one — the length of the minister's sermon on Sunday. It guarantees a full house! And if you've managed to make a deal with the minister on the side ... only joking!

---

[1] Martin Luther, *Exposition on Exodus 13:18*, in Plass (1496), as quoted in Ryken, *Work & Leisure in Christian Perspective*, IVP (1987).

Chapter Eight

TAKING GOD TO WORK

As dusk approaches Belinda begins to help the older guests to bed. She enjoys her work as a nurse in an old people's home and the old people appreciate her too. As each of them is tucked in, she says, 'Good night. God bless.' Her blessing is always reciprocated. It was not always like that. When Belinda first arrived, she thought she was just doing the job to earn some extra cash, because times were tough for her and Mark. However, she soon found that she not only enjoyed the job, but could meet various needs and sometimes see things that other staff missed. The 'Good night, God bless,' came naturally to her and was an encouragement to the residents. Some found it strange at first and one or two of the staff teased her about it. But today, all the guests and all the staff finish the day with a 'Good night, God bless'.

Belinda could leave her beliefs behind her at Crawley Community Church on a Sunday. Instead, she takes God to work with her. Strictly speaking, He's already there. But He manifests Himself through willing disciples who do not see work as something to get through as soon as possible, but who glorify Him in everything they do.

We have already said that work is far more than a mission field for the Christian employee. But we must not forget that we are also called to go to everyone and make disciples (Matt. 28:19–20). This is what Larry Tomczak calls 'the great commission, not the great suggestion'!

ON THE FRONT LINE

Christians in the workplace are as much on the front line as missionaries. In fact, because of the number of unbelievers that we are likely to meet, we are even more on the front line than ministers.

> Read Philippians 2:14–16 and note where Christians live.

> How can we be identified? (v. 15) What are we called to do? (vv. 14,16)

God is relying on us to offer life to those who are lost and caught up in sin. We are on the front line of God's army, establishing His Kingdom by the way we shine in our society. Let's look at some of the specific ways in which we can 'shine'.

PEACE AND CONTENTMENT

The prophet, Isaiah said:

> **'There is no peace', says the LORD, 'for the wicked' (Isa. 48:22).**

We must not be driven workaholics, or be lazy or careless. As we trust the real Boss in stressful situations, our composure will be evident to all. Our presence in the office, school or factory will make a difference. God is with us; He will see to it. His peace will radiate through us.

Along with peace comes contentment. We have already discussed some of the pressures in the workplace. As we deal successfully with these, God's light will shine through — even without our saying anything. Contentment will be evident in our attitude to the most mundane tasks. If we know that we are in the right place, we can deal with the temptations to be dissatisfied, to look for another job, to daydream. We will go beyond just 'putting up with the job' and actually learn to enjoy it. As we do this, our contentment will show and God will be glorified. In addition, the employer will benefit. He will soon realise that we are not caught up in the daily rat-race or exhausted by our own efforts.

Read Hebrews 4:9,10 and note the key to contentment in our work.

SERVICE

Our dependence on God, our worship of God and our service for
God will show through in a meekness, humility and dependability
in the tasks we undertake.

Think of different ways in which Jesus served during His
ministry on earth.

Read Mark 10:42–45; Luke 22:26–27 and John
13:4–5. Each passage deals with Jesus teaching and
examples of servanthood and service.

From these passages, set out the main principles of
service and apply them to your job.

**Do you see your work as serving your employer or
do you see your employer serving your needs?**

**Pray about ways of improving your service in
specific areas of your work.**

QUALITY

Andy is another member of our church at Crawley. All through the
toughest times of recession he has sought God for building,
painting and decorating work and has continued to receive it. He
has not always found it easy, but the jobs have always come in at
the right moment. The provision of work reflects not only Andy's
trust in God to provide, but also the quality of his work and the good
reputation that he has built up. He is not cheap to hire, but he is
always reliable, and invariably does a good job. In these days of
shoddy workmanship, Andy's witness lies in the care and hard
work he puts into every job. He honours God and God gives him
more work!

Read Ephesians 6:5–8 and note what our work qualities should be.

HONESTY

In these days of calling in sick when we are not, pilfering office supplies, and exaggerating company expenses, honesty is a valuable commodity to the employer. Whether or not people notice our honesty, God's light shines through. In fact, Scripture indicates that sooner or later, it will be noticed and draw others towards the truth:

Read Titus 2:9–10 and consider the way that honesty is depicted in this passage.

COMMITMENT AND LOYALTY

Not long ago there was a news story about a ship which sank off the South African coast. Fortunately, all were rescued. One of the amusing yet sad stories to come out of the episode concerned the captain. It seems that once the alarm had sounded, he was one of the first over the side. He did not exactly show much commitment or loyalty to his crew or to his job!

The same is true in the average company. Those driven by the god of self-fulfilment will not put loyalty to others on their priority list.

Taking this a stage further, if we prefer others and even let them get the credit for something we have done we will shock and surprise our fellow workers. Such behaviour just does not happen in the world and may often result in a positive response to our witness. As we operate according to the upside down gospel of the Kingdom and put others before ourselves, we will honour God and He will honour us (John 3:30; Luke 12:31).

LOVE

Influencing and affecting all of the above points is our love for God and our fellow employees. Jesus said:

> Love the Lord your God with all your heart and
> with all your soul and with all your mind. This is
> the first and greatest commandment. And the
> second is like it: Love your neighbour as yourself
> (Matt. 22:37–39).

All the law and the prophets hang on these, the greatest commandments. If it were not for God's love for us, we would not be reading this book. There would be no book to write.

> Read 1 Corinthians 13 and apply what is taught to
> your place of work.
>
> How can you apply each of the results of love (e.g.
> patience, kindness, lack of envy, etc.), to your daily
> work?
>
> Pray through each point.

**Thank God for His love for you, demonstrated by
His Son's death on the cross.**

**Compare the magnificence of this love with the love
that you are asked to show to your fellow employees.**

**Pray specifically for a work colleague whom you
don't particularly like or get on with.**

We are witnessing for God in all of the ways mentioned above — often without even opening our mouths. Let me finish this section by quoting Dr. David Cormack, a Christian management consultant. The extract is taken from a paper he presented to the British Institute of Management (which, of course, is not a Christian organisation):

Where does motivation come from? Where does trust, reliability, honesty, loyalty and a sense of community come from? – not from our skills but from our values and beliefs. What we see in the UK is not the result of a deficient skill base but of self-centred values. Our values have set manager against manager, department against department, customer against supplier and management against union ... The challenge to British managers is to rediscover the power of values and beliefs in the context of the workplace ... To run our businesses without reference to these fundamental concepts is like running a nuclear power station without the fuel rods — it's safer, but it never works very well![1]

SPEAKING UP

You're at a Sunday morning service. Your boss walks in and greets you with a hug. Joe, the company post boy, sits next to you. He's a new Christian and is so excited about Jesus. Samantha, the boss's secretary, has just received prayer following a terrible week in the office and is apologising to the boss for her reactions. We may dream that people at work will come to Christ through our testimony and be integrated into the local church. It is not an impossibility. With God, all things are possible (Mark 10:27). As we speak the words of life (Phil. 2:16; Heb. 4:12) God will take and use them to set captives free (Isa. 61:1).

It should be a privilege to be a spokesman for the God of the universe (2 Cor. 5:20). God wants us to look forward to sharing the gospel with others and to take each opportunity as it comes. Naturally, we are not primarily at work to witness, but it is important that we let people know what we believe. Let's run through some of the key points:

DON'T MISS OPPORTUNITIES

When we see that we are in partnership with God and that He calls us to do a particular work, we will begin to look forward to telling others about Him. Indeed, we will pray that opportunities to witness will come our way.

Many Christians treat work primarily as a hunting ground for potential converts. This false conclusion brings its own pressures. If our only reason for working is to win converts, what happens when opportunities to witness don't arise, or when we miss one of them? We feel guilty. If we measure our success in terms of the number of people we have led to Christ or how many tracts we have given out, what happens when no one responds either to Christ or to the offer of a tract? We feel a sense of failure.

Of course, there are always exceptions to this rule. Some are called to a job primarily to witness for Christ. More often than not, they are 'tentmakers'. Many of them take up a profession in a country where missionaries are unwelcome or where the preaching of the gospel is forbidden.

Work itself is a gift of God irrespective of whether we witness or not. When we realise this, we will be released from wrong motivation and guilt and set free to serve God and others to the best of our ability. It is not our responsibility to save people. God does that.

And yet, God chooses to work out His purposes through us. Having prevented the pendulum from swinging too far one way, we must be careful not to let it swing back too far. God wants us to speak to our colleagues about Christ, but to be motivated by love for Him, not a wrong understanding which declares, 'You ought to be witnessing.'

> Read Ephesians chapter 3 and consider our motivation in talking to our work colleagues about Christ.

Once our motivation is right we can look for every opportunity to share our faith. Colossians 4:5,6 encourages us to use every opportunity.

What else does the passage direct us to do?

The best way to use every opportunity is to be prepared and to build bridges:

BE PREPARED

'Be prepared' — the Scouts' motto could also be very suitable for the Christian in the workplace. It is exciting to work with God and to take full advantage of the opportunities He gives us to talk about Him.

If our workplace is not too far from our Sunday meeting place, one of the best ways to be prepared is to have a church leaflet or tract that we can give away as opportunities arise. I also carry a personal tract. This simply tells the reader how my wife, Roh, and I came to Christ. Larry Tomczak's book *Divine Appointments* (Kingsway) gives more detail on how to write a personal tract.

To illustrate the usefulness of personal tracts, let me tell you what happened to me. A few years ago, the Prime Minister of New Zealand resigned for health reasons and then there were various allegations about an affair that he was supposed to be having. On the day the story about the possible affair came to light, I found myself on the same plane as him. I reasoned that his resignation, ill health and need to confront the allegations were taking their toll on his life and prayed for an opportunity to speak to him.

Immediately the plane touched down at Auckland airport, he was whisked away by officials. I had missed my opportunity — or so I thought. As I walked from the domestic to the international terminal, I was praying for him and hoping that somehow I might still be able to meet him. I walked into the airport business lounge and there he was, pouring himself a coffee. Needless to say, I decided to have one too!

We got talking, mainly about the company I was working for, and at the end of the conversation, I produced my business card and personal tract. I asked if he would mind taking one of my 'family cards' as I call them (the front of the card has a photo of my family on it). I explained that I was a Christian and that the card would tell him more about Christ. He took it, read it, then put it into his pocket. I don't know if he has still got it, but I do know that on a day when he was having to face a number of serious issues, he had a card which pointed to the answers. That is just one instance of its use; there are many more. Be prepared.

BUILDING BRIDGES

Personally I am uneasy about directly challenging my fellow employees with the gospel. Unless they know me well, such an approach is likely to do more harm than good and put me into the 'religious cranks' category which will spoil any future witness. Usually I relate to my work colleagues in the same way as I do to my family. They have to put up with me all the time, so because of this, I try to be considerate in my relationships with them.

I maintain a silent witness and build bridges in conversation. If they notice any difference in the way I work, or are aware of my beliefs and begin asking questions, they will climb onto that bridge. To give a practical example: Often on a Monday morning the conversation will focus on what people got up to at the weekend. If I'm asked, I might say that I was worshipping with Christians the previous day. If anything significant happened such as a healing, I might mention that. I am building a bridge. If someone wants to climb onto it, he or she will start asking questions about the meeting. That might lead to an invitation to come along.

The problem with examples is that they are never quite that simple! Nevertheless, I think that bridge building is a good principle — particularly if it is backed up by personal prayer and the prayers of Christian friends (e.g. in the housegroup). These factors, combined with all round faithfulness at work will pave the way for God to move.

Read John 4:4–26 and consider the bridges that Jesus built for the Samaritan woman to climb on.

Think of bridges you might be able to build with your colleagues.

BACK-UP

Making the most of the opportunities, giving out personal tracts and building bridges all require a lot of behind the scenes back-up. We may need to pray and fast as individuals, and maybe even as housegroups. We must live what we preach and give a good proportion of time to social activities with our work colleagues (not for the sake of Kingdom gain, but because we are genuine friends with them).

To some extent we will always be nervous about speaking up for Christ — but that doesn't make it any the less a thrill or a privilege. Like Belinda, we may simply start with a 'Good night, God bless', or we may be able to explain the whole gospel. Whichever it is, God will use it to His glory. The picture of our boss and workmates worshipping alongside us need not be an unattainable dream.

---

[1] Dr. David Cormack, *Christian Herald*, 18 January, 1992. Used with permission.

Chapter Nine

BACK AT HOME BASE

A t the beginning of Chapter Two we left Peter sitting at his office desk on a Monday morning. He's learnt quite a lot since then. He's discovered that work is not a curse, but a blessing from God and has begun to apply what he has learned. As a result, the daily grind has been less of a grind. He is beginning to deal with the pressures of the job better and is becoming more ambitious. He is also more confident that his job is the right one for him and has started to relax and enjoy it. He no longer feels forced to witness — rather, he waits for natural openings and takes them in an unhurried way. As he approaches the weekend, he is in need of a well deserved rest. He places the urgent job in the centre of his desk for Monday morning and leaves the office looking forward to a relaxing weekend.

TIME OUT

American Football is not a game I am desperate to play. It's not only the bumps and bruises that deter me, it's the rules — and the gear! One thing I have learnt is that either team is allowed to call a 'time out' at various points in the game. This allows them to take a much needed breather and reconsider their strategy. This is exactly what workers must learn to do too.

ENJOYING THE REST

Jesus grew tired on many occasions (John 4:6) so we can safely say that tiredness is not a sin that should make us feel guilty. It is the natural outcome of a hard and satisfying day's work. Only when tiredness is caused by a wrong lifestyle (see Chapter Two) is there a problem. It is a delight to enjoy our rest as a response to tiredness.

> Read Mark 1:35 and consider what priority Jesus puts before rest.

> Read Psalm 132:3–5 and note what David's rest is dependent upon. How can we apply this to our lives?

> Read Psalms 46:10 and 131:2 and consider the result of David's time with God.

Time out with God is important — whether it is a few minutes spent in your room (Matt. 6:6), or a morning walking and enjoying God's creation (Ps. 121:1 -2). After a week in the daily grind, a staff meeting with our Heavenly Employer for refreshment and the resetting of priorities is essential.

Rest does not refer just to a specific time with God. A balance of work and leisure is very important too (see Chapter Five). It can be restful and relaxing to read a book, listen to music, pursue a hobby or dig the garden (unless you do it for a living!). Longer holiday breaks are also important. Although the holiday plans were rather interrupted by the crowds Jesus promotes this kind of idea in Mark.

> Then, because so many people were coming and going that they did not even have a chance to eat, he said to them, 'Come with me by yourselves to a quiet place and get some rest.' So they went away by themselves in a boat to a solitary place. But many who saw them leaving recognised them and ran on foot from all the towns and got there ahead of them (Mark 6:31–34).

BACK AT HOME BASE

ENJOYING THE FAMILY

Time out with the family is also important — particularly after a week at work when there has been little opportunity to be together. It leads to healthy family life.

Great stress is laid on a strong family unit in the Bible (Eph. 6:4, Titus 1:6). Activities which involve individual participation (e.g. board games, walking or sports) are preferable to those which involve little personal contact (e.g. watching TV). Playing a game or swimming together may not seem very restful, but the enjoyment of family life produces a wholeness and balances the activities of the week.

Parents need much wisdom and understanding to keep the right balance between work, church activities and family, but when the balance is right, the employer will benefit from a relaxed and productive employee. Where the employer insists on long hours and overtime to the exclusion of family life, the employee will never give his best. Communicating this fact to a workaholic boss may be a problem, but it is worthwhile trying. If he knows that you are a good worker and want the best for him and your family, he may be sympathetic to your request.

A CHURCH IN TOUCH

A supportive family, or partner if you are married, is important back-up to a productive working week. The role of the church is also vital. Time out with other believers is essential to the working Christian.

CENTRAL TO GOD'S PURPOSES

I am totally committed to the Church. It is central to God's purposes and must be seen in universal, local and practical terms. The person who says he is committed to the universal Church but does not need to be part of a local church is misreading Scripture (Acts 2:41–47, 1 Cor. 1:2, Eph. 2:22).

Because I believe in local church, I will be involved in it. Despite tiredness and business commitments, I will do my best to be at housegroup, prayer meetings and various other activities. But church activities do not constitute the church. We do not leave the meeting at the end of a Sunday morning and re-convene church on housegroup night. We are the Church. We are just as much the Church on Monday morning as we are Church on Sunday morning. Church should be central to our daily work.

CENTRAL TO DAILY WORK

If we are on the front line at work, then we are at headquarters when we are with the local church. A soldier returning to HQ will enjoy a rest and be encouraged and trained in the battle. Similarly, the Christian who returns to his church HQ will receive refreshment and advice which is relevant for day to day situations. Rest, encouragement, training and re-envisioning for the task are the responsibility of the local church.

> Read Ephesians 4:11-12. Consider the ministries
> that are given for the task and note the result of such
> ministries.

Sadly, there is often a lack of relevant teaching in the local church. While all Scripture is useful for teaching (2 Tim. 3:16), much instruction in the average congregation emphasises commitment to church based activities. It does not seem too relevant to people who need positive input for the battles that they face in their workplace.

A wonderful exception to this is the Te Atatu Bible Chapel in Auckland, New Zealand. Brian Hathaway, the Pastor, has geared the life of the church to the workplace. Members are encouraged to see their work as God given and therefore as an important part of their Christian lives. Brian views his congregation as front line troops who need equipping and refreshing before they go back to the front line on a Monday morning.

Brian's beliefs were tested when one of his elders was nominated as headmaster for the local school. At the time, the elders had been considering bringing him onto the full-time church staff. With Brian's encouragement, the man took the post of headmaster and gave up his church responsibilities. The church supports him in prayer as he battles on the front line for the lives of those school children. Sadly, Te Atatu is the exception rather than the rule.

THE LIE

Too many workers are being fed upon rather than fed. Church leaders often think that the godly individual is the one who attends most meetings and is most involved in church activities. They may not realise it, but in thinking that the full-time call is superior to the workplace call they have believed a lie and have introduced the sacred/secular divide. This may be the result of bad teaching or the poor example of others leaders. They emphasise church based activities to the detriment of church involvement in the workplace.

It is even likely that some people who are involved in church work should not be there. Once they may have wanted to do something for God and, because of their training, assumed that it had to be full-time work rather than a 'normal job'. So they believed the lie and launched into ministry. Now they feel like square pegs in round holes. They are unsatisfied with their work in the church but are afraid to return to the workplace because they think that a change from sacred to secular is demotion and not God's first choice.

The fruit of the lie is a workplace full of dissatisfied Christians, unable to enjoy what they do, waiting for the 'real work' to begin in the evenings and at weekends. Young people who take a year or two out to join, say, an evangelism team must be careful not to think that full-time Christian work is more godly than a 'normal job'. A Frontier Team can be a great adventure and produce men and women who are on fire for God. But the fire must be directed somewhere at the end of the year.

THE TRUTH

The truth is we are all full-time! The Bible does not speak of 'full-time Christian service'. In New Testament days it was accepted teaching that if you were a Christian, you were full-time. Nowhere is a new Christian encouraged to change his profession upon conversion — rather the opposite:

> Read 1 Corinthians 7:17–24 and consider how we should apply verses 20 and 24 to our work. What counts as more important than our circumstances?

The opportunity to go 'full-time' can seem very alluring, but it is not something Paul ever did on a permanent basis — however worthy of it he may have seemed. He taught the importance of working and then set the example by acting on his words.

> After this, Paul left Athens and went to Corinth. There he met a Jew named Aquila, a native of Pontus, who had recently come from Italy with his wife Priscilla, because Claudius had ordered all the Jews to leave Rome. Paul went to see them, and because he was a tentmaker as they were, he stayed and worked with them (Acts 18:1–3).

We need men and women who are willing to give their lives to serving the church. We need 'full-time' pastors. But we also need to redress the balance. As David Cormack has said:

> We are stewards of the resources of God in all aspects, but we have tended to emphasise the pastoral side rather than the physical, financial and organisational. So we tend to train our Christian leaders in ancient Greek and ancient

Hebrew. But there aren't a lot of ancient Greeks
and Hebrews around.[1]

If the truth is that we are all full-time, where are the young men
and women willing to dedicate their lives to serving God in the
workplace, willing to be salt and light, ready to be on the front line
for God? There is a battle waiting to be won out there. The enemy
intends the workplace to remain the breeding ground for the next
generation of the self-centred, indulgent and morally permissive.
God has other ideas. He is looking for a return to biblical absolutes
in the workplace and a fresh understanding of godly working
principles. Are we ready to fight and pray?

THE CHURCH IN ACTION

To overcome the lie, the church needs to be active in teaching and
applying the truth. We should look for:

An increased application of teaching and preaching to the daily
situations at work.

An increased emphasis on praying for work related situations.

Particular and regular encouragement and prayer for those in
responsible decision making jobs.

Discipleship of younger workers by those with many years'
experience in the workplace. Discipleship need not necessarily be
from the Pastor or housegroup leader since they may not have
much experience of workplace situations.

A place in the leadership or preferably, eldership, of the church
for mature Christians serving in the workplace. This will help
ensure that the local church keeps its feet firmly on the ground.

Church programmes that have active application to work.

Evangelism programmes that include teaching on work related
witnessing, not just open airs and door to door ministry.

In these, and many other ways, the local church can begin to
infiltrate the workplace, invading the world's darkness on a daily
basis. It may not seem a very glamorous task to love, listen to, pray

for and set examples to our colleagues in the workplace, but by God's grace they will bring lasting results.

In what careful and non provocative ways can you begin to encourage the leaders at your church to take a more serious look at the church's influence on the workplace?

Check out your own attitudes to 'normal jobs' and 'full-time' Christian work.

Although there is doubtless a place for 'parachurch' involvement in the workplace, the emphasis in Scripture is on the centrality of the church which finds expression through local congregations. Local church members in all their variety are best able to speak to workers. Where they have failed in the past, parachurch organisations have developed. Where such organisations are willing to work with local churches (and the local churches are awake enough for the need to do so) then so much the better.

> Consider how Ephesians 1:22–23 applies to the workplace.

When the Church invades the workplace, so does Christ. He is the head of the body (Col. 1:18). As individuals and churches let's be committed to Christ's vision for the workplace, pray for our members on the front line and train and encourage them in the battle. If there is that commitment, then Peter will be able to go to work on Monday morning with a smile on his face.

---

[1] Dr. David Cormack, *Alpha Magazine*, January 1992. Used with permission.

Chapter Ten

GOD PLC?

The business that God runs is bigger than any company world-wide. The workers He employs are active in every country around the globe. There are no national boundaries and no exchange controls. His activities are more diverse than the largest multinational. Products range from the stars of heaven to the smallest blood cell.

Central to His plan is man, His co-worker. The Christian has only one real Boss and whatever the product — nuts and bolts or nuts and raisins, stocks and shares or educated children — He is not only interested in it but is involved with us in it as well. God the worker set the example for man the co-worker. He is an architect, designing the tabernacle; a shipbuilder, preparing the ark; a farmer, owning the cattle on a thousand hills; an athlete, a teacher, a doctor, an artist, a writer — there is no limit to His skills, no end to His abilities. He is the ultimate creator.

God plc is an equal opportunities employer. The rewards are eternal and there's even a profit sharing scheme! In fact the only thing wrong with the title of this chapter is that it can never be a plc — a public limited company — because no one can limit God.

We started the book by looking at God the worker. We saw the effects of sin and the curse, and looked at God's answer to them. Then we applied the truth to our normal working lives. As we conclude, let's look more closely at the perfect worker, the best example of all.

THE PERFECT EXAMPLE

It seems clear from Scripture that in His early years, Jesus served His father in the carpenter's shop (Mark 6:3, Luke 2:40). Just as He obeyed His earthly father, so He obeyed His Heavenly Father.

THE FATHER'S WORK

Read Psalm 19:1 and Psalm 8:3–8.

Where is the work of the Father seen today? In what ways do men work for God?

Read John 4:34–36.

What work is Jesus to finish? In what way does Jesus extend man's work beyond that described in Psalm 8:3–8?

Jesus had a job to do. To use today's business language (which in this instance has more than a touch of Scripture about it), He had a clear mission statement: the will of the One who sent Him — nothing more, nothing less. Where Adam had failed, Jesus must succeed. His brief was to rule over God's work and put everything under His feet. (Ps. 8:6; see also 1 Cor. 15:25; Eph. 1:22). This was the Father's work for Him.

God blesses us with work, then shows us how to do it. How many of us have faced a difficult job with no clear idea of how to complete it? What we needed was someone to explain it to us. We serve God in our work by following the example of Jesus. So what example did He set?

DIGNITY AND DESTINY

Jesus did the Father's work with dignity. He was God's Son and knew exactly what His Father wanted Him to do. Nothing was too menial because it was done for the Father. So He washed men's feet (John 13:5); served a meal (Luke 9:16); cooked fish on an open fire (John 21:9) and hung on a cross and allowed men to spit on Him and beat Him. Whatever men did to Him, His identity never changed and He always did what pleased the Father.

If our work is God's work, we can also act with dignity. If our tasks seem mundane, we are still God's children and can approach our work with that in mind. When we face hard circumstances, we know Someone who has been there before us. And the price He paid in doing God's work puts our work difficulties into perspective. As we consider Him, we will joyfully work hard to His glory:

> Let us fix our eyes on Jesus, the author and perfecter of our faith, who for the joy set before him endured the cross, scorning its shame, and sat down at the right hand of the throne of God. Consider him who endured such opposition from sinful men, so that you will not grow weary and lose heart (Heb. 12:2–3).

Not only do we have a God given dignity, we have a God given destiny too. Jesus saw the end of the work. He knew what it would accomplish. It was worth getting through; worth the hardship; worth the cross.

If God has called us to our employment, then we too have a destiny in our work. Thankfully our job is unlikely to cost us our lives, although it will require endurance. No matter how much we may love our job, there will be times when it's hard, when there seem to be a few more thistles around and when the sweat on our brow is greater than usual (Gen. 3:17–19). Again, Jesus is our example. His destiny is ours. He wants us to produce fruit along the way and to finish the work.

FRUIT AND MORE FRUIT

Jesus bore fruit. There were tangible results from His day to day work. People were fed and healed and lives were changed. On one occasion, Jesus' work produced some excellent wine — fruit indeed (John 2:7–9)!

> Read 2 Thessalonians 2:17 and consider how God helps us bear fruit in our work.

> Read Ecclesiastes 5:18–20 and Colossians 1:10. How will fruitfulness bless us?

As we follow Jesus' example in our work, we will be fruitful. It may be seen by others, it may not. What matters is that God sees. Even before Jesus' public ministry, God saw all that His Son had done in the carpenter's shop and was able to say, 'this is my Son whom I love; with him I am well pleased' (Matt. 3:17).

Often we are blind to the fact that there is fruitfulness in our work simply because we are too close to the action. I once remember feeling fed up with church life. It was only when we went on holiday for a few weeks that I realised how much I missed our local church and how much I was taking it for granted. I had become so used to the fruit that I could no longer clearly see it.

Are you taking work for granted and not noticing the fruit that could be or is being produced?

In the context of your work, think of different ways you might be able to bear fruit.

Jesus was persecuted. As followers of Him, some of the 'fruit' that we produce will stir up aggression in others. Since we are an army of light invading the darkness, we must expect battles and opposition as well as success. Personally, I am quite pleased when I get a bit of healthy persecution. At least it means God is at work in the lives of my colleagues. Such reactions must be better than pure apathy!

FINISHED WORK

Not only did Jesus bear fruit in His life, He finished the work that
He started. He had a purpose and pressed on towards the goal
(Matt. 26:39–46).

> Read again John 4:34 and note the food that Jesus
> desires.
>
> Read John 2:22 and 10:32. What are the two results
> of Jesus' work?
>
> Read John 17:4. What is the result of the finished
> work?

Jesus finished the job. It was hard. It cost him His life. But He
made it. God was glorified; man was redeemed. By God's grace and
through the power of the Spirit, we can apply the finished work of
the cross to our own work. Only God knows all that we will
accomplish through our jobs. If we know that we are in the right
place, we will enjoy the good times, persevere in the hard times,
bring salt and light to the workplace and one day see the finished
work.

God has a destiny for us. It affects every area of our lives. He
is looking for people who will serve Him with dignity and work out
their destiny from day to day; for people who will finish the job that
they have started; for people who see that their employment is not
an inconvenience but a part of His overall plan.

As we let God work through us in His way, we can look forward
to the results. For Jesus, finishing the work meant sacrifice. He
faced the enemy head on and didn't flinch or give up. That's the
challenge for the Christian in the workplace. If we want fulfilment
in our lives, we will pray and work towards God's goals despite the
trials and challenges. And we will ignore the whisper of the enemy
who will try to persuade us that our daily work has no godly value.

A strong sense of purpose and destiny will ignite us and make us increasingly effective in our workplace. And as John Wesley once said, if we catch fire, people will come and watch us burn!

THE FINAL REVIEW

I can still recall my first company appraisal. I had spoken to the Director only a couple of times before I was invited into his office. As I sat down I remember staring at the paperweight on his desk and trying to block out all the fear and nervousness I was feeling. Then he spoke: 'Well done,' he said. I can't remember any of the rest. I was so relieved to hear those words, nothing else mattered!

APPRAISAL TIME

One day we will all have an appraisal of a rather final variety! (Rev. 20:11–12). How will the book of our life read? Will it be filled with works of service, or just Sunday services? Will the eighty thousand hours worked in an average lifetime figure at all in the final version or will the book be abridged because we treated our work as irrelevant?

We have only one life in this present world and we must use it to advance God's Kingdom. God wants to see His church back in the workplace, fulfilling His purposes as the world approaches its final appraisal. We have the privilege of being part of that church and of making every moment of our working day count.

Life is short. I began to realise how short when I recently played an album that I hadn't listened to for a while. The day I bought it seemed like yesterday. But the record was over twenty years old! Before long, this book will probably be gathering dust on a shelf. I should like to think that the majority of its readers didn't just agree with what it said, but actually put some of its teaching into practice.

Read 1 Peter 2:12.

What will be the eternal results of our work? What will be the temporal problems in our work?

Let's look again at a Scripture we mentioned earlier:

Whatever you do, work at it with all your heart, as working for the Lord, not for men, since you know that you will receive an inheritance from the Lord as a reward. It is the Lord Christ you are serving (Col. 3:23–24).

In view of this passage and the answers to the previous two questions, what must be our attitude to our work?

When you work, you are working for God. What will be your inheritance? What will be your reward? Will there be a 'well done' at that final appraisal?

Take time for an interim appraisal now. Check with your Heavenly Boss how He thinks you are matching up in reality to the answers you have given to the last three questions.

PREPARING THE BRIDE

The Church plays the main part in the final review. It is described as the bride of Christ, prepared and made ready at the end of time (Isa. 62:5; Rev. 19:7; 21:2,9). The final review is just prior to the marriage of the bride and bridegroom. Paul describes the Church at that time as having no spot or wrinkle — it is perfect (Eph. 5:27).

We are part of the bride, preparing ourselves for the bridegroom. We are not perfect yet, but as we allow God to touch our lives we will be more and more ready for the wedding day. Part of that preparation has to do with our daily work.

Each one of us has a part to play in the preparation of the bride. No part is too small. God looks on the heart rather than on the task that there are rewards in the new Kingdom (see also Eph. 6:7–8). This is further illustrated by Jesus in the parable of the talents: Matt. 25:14–30.

Read the passage for yourself.

The parable is about God's judgement and the giving of rewards in eternity. We have seen that work was here before the curse. It seems likely therefore, that there will be work of some sort in the new heaven and earth.

What do you think will be the major differences between today's work and work in the new Kingdom?

THE FINAL, FINAL REVIEW!

In Chapter One, you looked at a set of statements and assessed your work in the light of them. The statements are again set out below. This time respond to them with a bit of faith and vision from what you have learned:

Most of the time my job is boring. I feel unfulfilled and underused.

I can't get excited about what I do. My job seems irrelevant to the world out there.

I hate my job. I would gladly give up tomorrow if I didn't have to pay the bills.

I enjoy what I do but find it difficult to see how God fits into it.

I don't enjoy my job much but am beginning to see that God is working with me.

I enjoy my job and am beginning to find ways of sharing my faith and of bringing God into my daily routines.

My job is fantastic. I feel totally fulfilled and couldn't think of any way of improving what I do.

Hopefully we can relate to some of the latter statements here. In this imperfect world, the last one is probably reserved for eternity!

Christianity is more than Sunday attendance or even Sunday plus other meetings plus, perhaps, family. God is interested in all our daily life. He has plans for our workplace. It is time to redeem our working hours, step out in faith and see what God will do.

Let Jesus' words in the parable of the talents be your final encouragement:

> Well done good and faithful servant! You have been faithful with a few things; I will put you in charge of many things. Come and share your master's happiness! (Matt. 25:21)

For Further Reading

Doug Sherman & William Hendricks, *Your Work Matters to God*, NavPress (1987).
> A thorough and readable guide to all aspects of work today.

Larry Peabody, *Secular Work is Full-Time Service*, CLC (1974).
> Useful as a short introduction for Christians in the workplace from a biblical standpoint.

Leland Ryken, *Work & Leisure in Christian Perspective*, IVP (1987).
> Covers leisure issues as well as work. Includes a well researched history of Christian attitudes to work.

David Frahm with Paula Rinehart, *The Great Niche Hunt*, NavPress (1991).
> Particularly useful for those considering a career change.

Myron Rush, *Management: A Biblical Approach*, Victor Books (1988).
> As the title suggests, the book contains some excellent teaching on management.